William Hartston, an International Master and twice winner of the British Chess Championship, is a chess journalist and broadcaster, and an industrial psychologist. He is well known to television audiences for his commentaries on the BBC2 series *The Master Game* and *World Chess Report*, and the children's series, *Play Chess*. His publications range from serious works on chess opening theory to the light-hearted *How to Cheat at Chess* and *Soft Pawn*.

W. R. HARTSTON

Karpov *v* Korchnoi

The World Chess Championship 1981

FONTANA PAPERBACKS

First published by Fontana Paperbacks 1981

Copyright © W. R. Hartston 1981

Set in Linotron Times by
Western Printing Services Ltd, Bristol
Made and printed in Great Britain by
William Collins Sons & Co. Ltd, Glasgow

Contents

Foreword

The match in Merano between Anatoly Karpov and Viktor Korchnoi was more than just a series of chess games to decide the World Championship. To understand the significance of the event, an appreciation is necessary of the characters of the participants, the role of chess in the Soviet Union and the impact of the match on those chessplayers and casual bystanders who were caught by its irresistible impact on the small Italian Tyrolean town which had been selected as venue.

I felt myself to be too involved in the world of chess to be able to write with total objectivity on the impression made on Merano by an invasion of chessmasters, so I was very grateful when Peter Jay, poet, translator and keen chessplayer himself, offered to contribute a chapter of his own observations made during a visit to the scene of the match.

In my analyses of the games, I have cause to be grateful to Raymond Keene and Helmut Pfleger with whom I had the opportunity to discuss several of the critical positions during our television recordings. For my section on chess in the USSR, I have drawn deeply from the excellent work, *Soviet Chess* by D. J. Richards (Oxford University Press 1965), which I thoroughly recommend to anyone who requires an authoritative version of the subject.

W. R. HARTSTON

ANATOLY KARPOV
The World Champion

During the great tournament of Moscow 1925, three Russian psychologists took advantage of the presence of so many of the world's
greatest chessplayers to perform a series of tests and experiments
designed to identify the qualities necessary for success at chess. Their
results were published the following year in a booklet entitled 'The
Psychology of Chess' by I. N. Dyakov, N. V. Petrovsky and P. A.
Rudik. The central conclusion was embodied in a chess masters'
psychogram which consisted of sixteen physical and psychological
qualities found to be characteristic of the great players. Eight of these
factors relate to the mental abilities needed for the game. The other
eight are the following:

i   A good reserve of physical strength and good general health.
ii   Strong nerves.
iii Self-control.
iv Combative ability.
v   A disciplined will.
vi   A highly active intellect.
vii Disciplined emotions.
viii Self-confidence.

One could hardly ask for a better description of Anatoly Karpov.
Apart from some slight doubts on the first of these factors ('He is too
thin to be a grandmaster' was one early misjudgment of the young
Karpov's potential) the World Champion is a model of the psychologists' formula. His chess style, the inexorable progress of his career
and even his attitude at the chessboard all reflect that highly controlled, stable and determined character which the above recipe demands.

Meeting Karpov away from the chessboard, one could be excused
for failing to be impressed. He is quiet, unforthcoming and hard to get
to know well. He treats most strangers with a somewhat suspicious air
and rarely overcomes his natural reticence to utter more than politely

9

bland replies to their questions. Despite this taciturnity, or more likely because of it, Karpov has earned considerable respect as a chess diplomat. Ever tactful, the World Champion has regained for chess that polished, gentlemanly image which was so tarnished by the publicity surrounding recent World Championship matches.

At the chessboard, Karpov assumes a powerfully impressive image. He plays quickly and with a confidence which seems almost arrogant in its speed of decision. After his move, he will remain seated at the board, thinking in his opponent's time until he is happy about his next move also. Then he will rise from his chair and walk around, looking bored until his opponent has replied. Rarely does he look at all worried about the position. His preparation, particularly in some of his favourite opening variations, is so deep that many of his most impressive games are simply the implementation of ideas fully worked out away from the tensions of match or tournament. In such games he will appear to consume little time or energy; all the hard work has already been done. The game itself is just a piece of professional technique.

This air of certainty which seems to accompany Karpov to the board is understandable in a man whose chess career has been totally free from serious setbacks. His progress through the ranks of Master, Grandmaster and Candidate to World Champion was accomplished without delays, surmounting each obstacle at the first opportunity. Only Mikhail Tal before him had swept aside all opposition so easily, but he only held on to the title for a single year. Karpov's unique achievement has been to continue to improve in both play and results after reaching the highest level.

Anatoly Yevgenyevich Karpov was born on 23 May 1951 in the town of Zlatoust, an industrial centre in the Urals almost a thousand miles east of Moscow. He learnt to play chess before he was five years old and made such quick progress that he had attained the rank of Candidate Master by the age of eleven. This achievement marked the young Anatoly as a player of extreme promise; there had never been so young a Candidate Master in the Soviet Union. He was duly selected for special training at the chess school of former World Champion Mikhail Botvinnik in Moscow. One session at the school took the form of a clock simultaneous display, Botvinnik playing against six promising youngsters. The game with Karpov sees the old grandmaster mesmerizing his young opponent with subtle opening play, completely outplaying him in the early middlegame, establishing a totally winning position . . . then blundering his queen away. Karpov immediately blundered back and the game staggered to a draw. Botvinnik is quoted as saying of Karpov after this game: 'He doesn't understand anything about chess.' In Karpov's official biography the story of the game is elaborated with the young Candidate Master suggesting that Botvinnik retract his blunder; when the grandmaster refused to do so, Karpov insisted on blundering back, refusing to gain an 'unlawful' point. Here are the the moves of this historic encounter. Readers may judge for themselves.

White: A. Karpov Black: M. M. Botvinnik
Caro–Kann Defence

1 P–K4 P–QB3 2 P–Q4 P–Q4 3 N–QB3 P–KN3 4 N–B3 B–N2 5 B–KB4 B–N5 6 P×P P×P 7 N–QN5 K–B1!? 8 P–KR3 (*8 N–B7 would have been met by P–K4!*) 8 . . . B×N 9 Q×B N–QB3 10 P–B3 N–B3 11 B–Q3 P–QR3 12 N–R3 Q–N3 13 Q–K2 N–KR4 14 B–K3 Q–B2 15 0–0 N–B5 16 Q–Q2 N×B 17 Q×N P–KR4 18 N–B2 B–B3 19 P–KB4? (*After this the white squares become very weak and the bishop bad*) 19 . . . P–K3 20 N–K1 P–R5 21 N–B3 N–K2 22 N–K5 N–B4 23 B–B1 K–N2 24 R–B2 B–K2 25 Q–B3 P–QN4 26 B–Q2 P–N5 27 R–K2 P–R4 28 QR–K1 R–QR3 29 Q–Q3 Q–N2 30 R–QB1 R–QB1 31 B–K1 P–R5 32 P–B4 N×P! 33 R–Q2 (*Of course 33 Q×N loses the queen to B–B4*) 33 . . . N–B4 34 R(2)–QB2 N–K6! 35 R–K2 P×P 36 N×QBP N×N 37 R×N R–Q3 38 Q–K4 R×R?? 39 Q×Q B–B3 40 B×NP? B–Q5+ 41 K–R2 R–N3 42 Q–K7 R(B5)×B agreed drawn.

Karpov naturally continued his school studies while maintaining his chess progress. He was a good student, especially in mathematics, and qualified for a place in the Faculty of Mathematics and Mechanics at Moscow University. 'I studied for a year, and saw that chess and mathematics were incompatible.' So he switched to economics. But already it was clear that Karpov's career was to be chess. Even at the age of fifteen he had won first place in an international tournament. That had been in Třinec, Czechoslovakia, but was all a huge accident, since the Soviet representatives had been nominated under the misapprehension that the invitations were for a junior event. Undeterred to discover that he had arrived at a full adult competition, Karpov dominated the event to win with 11/13, conceding only four draws.
  The next few years in Karpov's tournament life passed as though he

were following a pre-ordained career path leading straight to the World Championship: European Junior Champion in 1968, World Junior Champion in 1969, he was already tipped as the outstanding young player in the world. He gained his grandmaster title in Caracas in 1970 by finishing fourth in a strong grandmaster tournament. His play had already acquired a polished maturity and a professional solidity which ensured that defeats were rare. High placings in Soviet Championships confirmed his arrival among the world's elite, but Karpov's outstanding performance in the Alekhine Memorial Tournament in Moscow at the end of 1971 still surprised even his greatest admirers. The twenty-year-old Karpov shared first place with Leonid Stein, without losing a game, ahead of such great players as Smyslov, Petrosian, Spassky, Tal, Bronstein and Hort. Korchnoi was only able to manage eleventh place.

Most great players, even after they have reached the ranks of the top dozen in the world, need some years of hard competition before they learn how to win the strongest tournaments, rather than simply being satisfied with high placings. Karpov needed no such apprenticeship. He travelled directly from Moscow to Hastings and there secured another share of first prize, this time halving the spoils with Korchnoi.

The Hastings tournament was the first occasion on which the strong personal animosity between Karpov and Korchnoi was on view to the general public. Korchnoi clearly felt that the young pretender ought not yet to be winning tournaments ahead of the world's leading grandmasters. But Karpov raced away to a clear lead in the event, to Korchnoi's evident annoyance. When they met in the penultimate round, Korchnoi badly needed a win if he was to avoid finishing behind the young upstart. His pleasure after the game was undisguised.

White: V. Korchnoi   Black: A. Karpov
Torre Attack

1 P–Q4 N–KB3 2 N–KB3 P–K3 3 B–N5 P–QN3 4 P–K4 P–KR3
5 B×N Q×B 6 B–Q3 B–N2 7 QN–Q2 P–Q3 8 Q–K2 P–QR3 9 0–
0–0 N–Q2 10 K–N1 P–K4 11 P–B3 B–K2? (*This leaves the black queen exposed and cut off on KB3; instead the preparatory 11 . . . Q–Q1 was better.*) 12 N–B4 0–0 13 B–B2 KR–K1 14 P–Q5 P–B4? (*Another poor decision; Black should try to open the game with 14 . . . P–B3*) 15 N–K3 B–KB1 16 P–KN4! Q–Q1 17 P–N5! P–KR4 (*17 . . . P×P 18 QR–N1 with P–KR4 to follow, gives White a*

tremendous attack) 18 P–N6! P×P 19 KR–N1 Q–B3 20 N–N5 B–K2 21 N–K6 N–B1 (*Giving up the exchange rather than submit to the attack after 21 . . . QR–B1 22 R–N2 N–B1 23 QR–N1, but Black's game now becomes hopeless*) 22 N–B7 Q–B2 23 QR–KB1 P–QN4 24 N×QR B×N 25 P–QB4 R–N1 26 B–Q3 Q–K1 27 R–B1 B–KB3 28 R–N2 R–N3 29 QR–N1 R–N1 (*White threatened 30 R×P N×R 31 Q×P*) 30 Q–B1 P–N5 31 B–K2 P–R5 32 R×P! Q×R (*After 32 . . . N×R 33 B–R5 White wins quickly on the white squares*) 33 R×Q N×R 34 B–N4 N–B5 35 Q–Q1 P–N6 36 P×P B–N2 37 N–N2! B–B1 (*37 . . . N×N 38 B–K6+ and 39 Q–R5 wins at once for White*) 38 B×B R×B 39 Q–N4 R–K1 40 N×N P×N 41 Q×BP B–K4 42 Q×P R–KB1 43 P–N4 B–Q5 44 P×P resigns.

In 1972 came an event which had a profound significance for Karpov's career: Bobby Fischer defeated Boris Spassky for the World Championship. The effect on Soviet chess was dramatic. Not only Spassky but all of his generation were discredited. They were accused of taking life too easily and enjoying themselves in international tournaments instead of working to maintain standards. A strict regime was imposed, insisting on more hard competitive events within the USSR for those players who wished to compete internationally. Above all, the young players were to be given every opportunity to replace the old generation. Suddenly it was noticed that the leading players were all aged over thirty-five; Spassky, Petrosian, Tal and Korchnoi had not been followed by an equally promising group of youngsters. The only player who seemed to have any chance of regaining the World Championship for the USSR was the young Karpov. Even as early as 1972, with Spassky and Petrosian still suffering from the effects of their defeats by the American, Karpov was being mentioned as a possible challenger in 1975. And his run of successes did everything to encourage those who supported his endeavours. At the end of 1972 he added still further to his reputation by sharing first place at San Antonio with Petrosian and Portisch ahead of Gligoric, Keres, Hort and Larsen among others.

By now everyone was looking forward to the qualifying tournaments for the World Championship. In the Interzonal in Leningrad 1973, the Karpov–Korchnoi rivalry gained impetus as the two of them raced away from the field to share first place with 13½/17. Karpov was the only undefeated player in the tournament. The third qualifying place for the Candidates matches was taken, surprisingly, by the

American grandmaster Robert Byrne. Among those falling by the wayside were Larsen, Tal and Hübner.

The next hurdle to surmount was the first serious match of Karpov's career (though he had played a training match with Korchnoi in 1971). The draw for the Candidates paired him against Polugayevsky, an experienced grandmaster renowned for his intensive theoretical preparation. Karpov lost several of the disputes in the openings but always seemed capable of drawing his inferior positions with the black pieces and winning the equal games he obtained with white. The final score was a 3–0 win to Karpov with five draws. Polugayevsky had certainly had his chances in the match, but victory always eluded him.

The next match was a sterner test. Karpov had to meet Spassky, who was still the favourite to secure another chance to meet Fischer. After the first game, Karpov's chances looked slim. He had been routed with the white pieces by an energetic attacking game from the former World Champion. But this was to be Spassky's last success of the match. Karpov quickly settled into his normal calm routine and it became clear that Spassky was the player lacking in confidence and less well equipped with new ideas. Karpov equalized in game three, took the lead in game six (with a quiet positional victory as Black in a Caro-Kann defence) and finally destroyed Spassky's remaining resistance with a superb victory in the ninth game:

White: A. Karpov   Black: B. Spassky
Sicilian Defence

1 P–K4 P–QB4 2 N–KB3 P–K3
3 P–Q4 P×P   4 N×P N–KB3
5 N–QB3 P–Q3   6 B–K2 B–K2
7 0–0 0–0   8 P–B4 N–B3   9 B–
K3 B–Q2 10 N–N3 P–QR4 11 P–
QR4 N–QN5   12 B–B3 B–B3
13 N–Q4 P–KN3 14 R–B2 P–K4
15 N×B P×N   16 P×P P×P
17 Q–KB1 Q–B1 18 P–R3 N–Q2
19 B–N4 P–R4   20 B×N Q×B
21 Q–B4 B–R5 22 R–Q2 Q–K2
23 R–KB1 KR–Q1 (*see diagram*)

24 N–N1! (*An outstanding move which exposes all the deficiencies in Black's position. The knight on N5 has no good retreat, the QB–pawn is*

weak and the KP also vulnerable if the white knight travels to KB3 via Q2) 24 . . . Q–N2 25 K–R2! *(Another fine move, threatening to win the bishop with P–KN3)* 25 . . . K–N2 26 P–B3 N–R3 27 R–K2! *(freeing Q2 for the knight)* 27 . . . R–KB1 28 N–Q2 B–Q1 29 N–B3 P–B3 30 R–Q2 B–K2 31 Q–K6 *(The final invasion begins; Black has no good defence to the threat of R–Q7)* 31 . . . QR–Q1 32 R×R B×R *(or 32 . . . R×R 33 N×P! P×N 34 R–B7+)* 33 R–Q1 N–N1 34 B–B5 R–R1 35 R×B! resigns *(since 35 . . . R×R 36 B–K7 gives White a mating attack).*

After that game, Spassky crashed to an even more disastrous defeat in game eleven and the match was over, 4–1 to Karpov with six draws.

The final match of the Candidates was between Korchnoi and Karpov at the end of 1974. This was a bitter encounter, since Korchnoi believed that the Soviet chess authorities were giving Karpov every possible help to ensure his victory. More of that match elsewhere in this book; suffice it to record that Karpov emerged the narrow winner to earn the right to play Bobby Fischer. But Bobby would not come out to play. He had not played since he defeated Spassky in 1972, and once again he was unable to bring himself to agree to the rules for a defence of his title. So, on 24 April 1975, after various deadlines for Fischer had come and gone, Anatoly Karpov was formally crowned World Chess Champion, the twelfth holder of that title since its inauguration in 1886.

Perhaps his succession to the title by default spurred Karpov on to become the most successful World Champion since Alekhine. Every other title holder had apparently relaxed after gaining the highest honour, and since the Second World War it had been rare to see a tournament won by the World Champion. Karpov changed all that. He still had a great deal to prove, since many only grudgingly accepted him as champion. He had to demonstrate that he was as worthy a holder as Fischer, by playing in the strongest tournaments and winning them.

During the next three years, Karpov regained for the title of World Champion a respect it had not been accorded for almost half a century. With eight outright tournament victories and another shared first place in eleven events between 1975 and 1978, Karpov dominated the world chess scene. By the time he had to defend his title, he was the undisputed king. Fischer had not played for six years and was virtually forgotten. The only challenge came from the rejuvenated Viktor Korchnoi.

His shaky victory in Baguio City in 1978 left Karpov exhausted. He did not play in another tournament for more than five months. But when he did, his winning ways immediately resumed. He shared first place (with Tal) in the very strong Montreal tournament in 1979, then went on to take first prizes at Tilburg 1979, Bugojno 1980, Amsterdam 1980 and Tilburg 1980, all of these tournaments of the highest class. The only suggestion of any possible weakness in Karpov's play during this period was an apparent vulnerability in opening systems which he had not prepared well. At Montreal, Larsen had defeated him as Black in a game which began 1 P–K4 P–Q4 2 P×P Q×P. In the European Team Championship in 1980, he had lost a game with an even more bizarre opening:

White: A. Karpov   Black: A. J. Miles

1 P–K4 P–QR3!? 2 P–Q4 P–QN4 3 N–KB3 B–N2 4 B–Q3 N–KB3 5 Q–K2 P–K3 6 P–QR4 P–B4 7 QP×P B×BP 8 QN–Q2 P–N5 9 P–K5 N–Q4 10 N–K4 B–K2 11 0–0 N–QB3 12 B–Q2 Q–B2 13 P–B4 P×P e.p. 14 N×P N×N 15 B×N N–N5 16 B×N B×B 17 QR–B1 Q–N3 18 B–K4 0–0 19 N–N5 P–R3 20 B–R7+ K–R1 21 B–N1 B–K2 22 N–K4 QR–B1 23 Q–Q3? (*White's curious mixture of hesitancy and aggression has given him no advantage, but this move is an outright blunder, losing at least a pawn*) 23 . . . R×R 24 R×R Q×P 25 R–K1 Q×P 26 Q×QP B–N5 27 R–K3 Q–Q4 28 Q×Q B×Q 29 N–B3 R–B1 30 N–K2 P–N4 31 P–R4 K–N2 32 P×P P×P 33 B–Q3 P–R4 34 R–N3 K–B3 35 R–N4 B–Q3 36 K–B1 B–K4 37 K–K1 R–KR1 38 P–B4 P×P 39 N×P B–B3 40 N–K2 R–R8+ 41 K–Q2 R–R7 42 P–N3 B–B6 43 R–N8 R–N7 44 K–K1 B×N 45 B×B R×P 46 R–QR8 B–B2 White resigned.

Karpov was annoyed after this game at the rudeness of Black's choice of opening, but Miles's decision can also be seen as a compliment to Karpov's mastery of conventional opening systems. When strong grandmasters cannot find a standard opening line which they are prepared to defend against the World Champion, his technique must be regarded with supremely high respect. And rightly so, of course. Let us conclude this section with a typical Karpov victory, a pure strategic win which took him less than an hour and a half on the clock.

White: A. Karpov   Black: W. Unzicker
Nice Chess Olympics, 1974.

1 P–K4 P–K4 2 N–KB3 N–QB3 3 B–N5 P–QR3 4 B–R4 N–B3 5 0–0 B–K2 6 R–K1 P–QN4 7 B–N3 P–Q3 8 P–B3 0–0 9 P–KR3 N–QR4 10 B–B2 P–B4 11 P–Q4 Q–B2 12 QN–Q2 N–B3 13 P–Q5 N–Q1 14 P–QR4 R–N1 15 P×P P×P 16 P–QN4 (*White's strategy is eventually to push forward on the K-side with P–KB4, but first he wants to induce Black to play P–QB5 in order that after P–KB4, the capture KP×P will free the square Q4 for a white knight*) 16 . . . N–N2 17 N–B1 B–Q2 18 B–K3 R–R1 19 Q–Q2 KR–B1 20 B–Q3 P–N3 21 N–N3 B–B1 22 R–R2 P–B5 (*At last Black gives in and plays this advance, but the alternative was to allow KR–R1 with White control of the QR-file*) 23 B–N1 Q–Q1

24 B–R7! (*blocking the file to allow White time to bring his KR to QR1*) 24 . . . N–K1 25 B–B2 N–B2 26 KR–R1 Q–K2 27 B–N1 B–K1 28 N–K2 N–Q1 29 N–R2 B–N2 30 P–B4! P–B3 (*Passive, but 30 . . . P×P 31 N×P leaves the other white knight coming to KB3 and Q4*) 31 P–B5 P–N4 32 B–QB2 B–B2 33 N–N3 N–N2 34 B–Q1 P–R3 35 B–R5 Q–K1 36 Q–Q1 N–Q1 37 R–R3 K–B1 38 R(1)–R2 K–N1 39 N–N4 K–B1 (*Capturing twice on KR4 would lose the queen to N×BP+*) 40 N–K3 K–N1 41 B×B+ N×B 42 Q–R5 N–Q1 43 Q–N6 K–B1 44 N–R5 resigns. (*The white square invasion is complete; the other knight comes to KN4 or to KB5 if Black exchanges queens and all is soon over.*)

Such masterpieces of precision and control are the hallmark of Karpov's style. His play may not have the brilliant flamboyance of a Tal or a Fischer, but for sheer efficiency he is already established as one of the greatest players in the history of the game.

VIKTOR KORCHNOI
The Challenger

At fifty years of age, Viktor Korchnoi, by all precedents, ought not to be challenging for the World Chess Championship. Quinquagenarians have contested matches for the title before, but never in the role of pretender, bidding to oust the sitting champion. The effect of aging on chess ability is difficult to understand, but all statistics indicate that grandmasters reach their peak around the age of thirty, maintain the same level for up to ten years, then begin a gradual decline. Skill at chess is a blend of experience and mental stamina, so perhaps this is only to be expected. As the grandmaster ages, his experience and knowledge of the game increase, but his capacity to work hard at the board deteriorates, tiredness becomes an increasing problem, and results gradually begin to suffer.

So how does Korchnoi do it? The secret seems to lie in two factors: intensive physical preparation, to insure against fatigue; and an abnormally high level of motivation. The will to win is an essential part of the composition of any chessplayer, but in Korchnoi's case it reaches the level of an obsession. In an article on chess style, published in *Shakhmaty v SSSR* in 1936, the author, L. Spokoiny, characterized two types of player:

> . . . players for whom the essence of the game is the element of struggle, for whom each game is played with the specific opponent in mind, and on the other hand players who are convinced that each position and each problem arising on the board are so subject to objective logic that the individual physiognomy of the opponent is unimportant . . .

He called these two types 'psychologists' and 'classicists'; others have called them fighters and players. Korchnoi is an excellent example of the first type, a fighter in whose hands the chess pieces are a weapon with which to destroy the man sitting opposite. Though he would be loath to describe himself as such, Korchnoi might be considered a model Soviet chessplayer. As Spokoiny went on to write: 'The Soviet style of chess is characterized by its aggressiveness . . . the main characteristic of the Soviet style is the element of struggle. . . .' The two other players who were still battling for the World Championship in their fifties were Lasker and Botvinnik. For them, too, chess was a struggle above all else. What the three veteran prodigies seem to have proved is that chess skill need not deteriorate as long as the will to fight remains alive. In Korchnoi's case, the fact that he has never yet won the World Championship contributes greatly to his need to keep going. He has seen the rivals of his youth, Tal, Spassky and Petrosian, all succeed. He still believes that his turn will come.

Korchnoi's chessplaying career began in Leningrad, the city of his birth. Like many of his generation, he was spared the responsibility of being a child prodigy by the intervention of the Second World War. Born on 23 April 1931 (though for no clear reason Russian sources always give the date as 23 July), Viktor Lvovich Korchnoi was already fifteen years old by the time organized chess regained its momentum. His earliest recorded games are from the USSR Junior Championships of 1946 and 1947, both of which were held in his home city. He won the latter event, but in those faraway days there were no international junior tournaments so Korchnoi had to continue the laborious climb up the ladder of Soviet chess. In 1952 he succeeded for the first time in qualifying for the final of the Soviet Championship, at that time probably the strongest tournament in the world. He confirmed his promise by taking sixth place, ahead of, among others, Bronstein, Smyslov and Keres. In the following USSR Championship, played at the beginning of 1954, Korchnoi improved his position to share second place. This result earned him his first trip abroad, to play at Bucharest 1954. His first place at that tournament marked his arrival on the international scene. For the next few years, mixed results in the Soviet Union were interspersed with international successes on the rare occasions he was nominated to participate abroad. A shared first at Hastings 1955–6 was followed by first place at Krakow 1959, but he played only in events inside the USSR during the intervening years (apart from the occasional team tournaments).

During the 1960s Korchnoi finally broke through to the forefront of world masters. Beginning with the strong international tournament in Buenos Aires 1960, where he shared first place with Reshevsky, Korchnoi began a run of successes. He was selected for the Soviet team in the Olympiad of the same year, when he made the fine score of $10\frac{1}{2}$/13 on fourth board. What must have given Korchnoi greater pleasure, however, was his second place in the 1961 USSR Championship, because that event was also a qualifying tournament for the Interzonal. Korchnoi gained one of the four coveted places, leaving such players as Smyslov, Spassky, Polugayevsky and Bronstein having to wait three years before they could try again.

He celebrated by an outstanding first place at Budapest 1961. This was to be the first of many international tournaments won by Korchnoi by a large margin over the player in second place. Most grandmasters appear happy to finish first; already it was clear that Korchnoi would only be truly content if he won every game. His score at Budapest was 11½/16, two points ahead of Filip and Bronstein. More impressive victory margins in later events were, for example, at Leningrad 1964 (four points ahead of the second prize winner), Gyula 1965 (five and a half points!), Bucharest 1966 (two and a half points), and Wijk aan Zee 1968 (three points ahead of Tal, Portisch and Hort).

By taking fourth place in the Interzonal tournament at Stockholm 1962, Korchnoi qualified for his first Candidates event. Eight players were each to meet four times to decide who would have the right to challenge Mikhail Botvinnik for the World Championship. Korchnoi started well and was leading after the first quarter of the tournament, but in the words of Petrosian's biographer, V. Vasiliev: 'Korchnoi must burn himself out. No man could continue to expend such colossal amounts of physical and nervous energy in every game.' The second quarter was moderate for Korchnoi, but the third was disastrous. Three losses left him totally out of contention and he had to be content with fifth place.

He had to wait six years for another chance, because in 1964 he was eliminated from the World Championship at the USSR Zonal stage. He occupied his time winning several tournaments and two Soviet championships before qualifying for the Candidates again from the Interzonal at Sousse 1967. By that time the rules had changed the Candidates from a tournament into a series of matches. In the quarter-finals Korchnoi was drawn against Reshevsky, the veteran United States grandmaster. The match was scheduled over ten games, but only eight were necessary before Korchnoi romped home 5½–2½. He had been unstoppable with the white pieces, playing 1 P–K4 in the first game, 1 N–KB3 in game three and 1 P–QB4 in game five; he won all of them.

This qualified him for a match with his old rival, Mikhail Tal. Tal had always had difficulties in his games against Korchnoi. This match followed the pattern and Korchnoi won 5½–4½. So Korchnoi was within one match of a crack at the World Championship; only Boris Spassky stood in his way. But Spassky was too strong. In a match of heavy strategic games, Korchnoi was beaten convincingly by a score of 6½–3½.

For a long time it looked as though this would be the nearest Korchnoi would get to the World Champsionship. In the next cycle, he lost in the semi-finals to Petrosian. That was a strange match in which Petrosian appeared content to draw every game until, in sheer frustration, Korchnoi gave him the opportunity to win the ninth.

Korchnoi gained his revenge three years later at the same stage of the Candidates matches. Petrosian was no longer the immovable object he had been, and Korchnoi won a very bad-tempered match 3½–1½, with Petrosian walking out before the scheduled finish. This was the match which brought into chess allegations of ungentlemanly conduct and kicking under the table. Once again Korchnoi had reached the final, but it looked as though there would always be someone to bar his path. In the old days it had been Petrosian or Spassky; now the younger generation had swept through in the form of Karpov. The games of that match are discussed elsewhere in this book, but its aftermath had great repercussions for Korchnoi's career and, indeed, his whole life.

Korchnoi had never had an easy relationship with the Soviet chess authorities. He was too much an individualist to accept their discipline willingly. Matters came to a crisis around the time of the Karpov–Korchnoi match in 1974. When the Soviet Chess Federation was trying to build up the image of Karpov as a credible World Champion, Korchnoi announced it his duty to try to save their young star from having to meet Fischer. This and other criticisms of Karpov's chess abilities published by Korchnoi earned him a year's suspension from travelling to foreign tournaments.

Korchnoi realized that he faced the threat of his career being brought to an untimely end. He began to think of leaving the Soviet Union. Indeed, he spoke so openly about his plans for defection that it was difficult to believe he could seriously be considering the action. During the tournament at Amsterdam 1976, after asking other players how to pronounce the word 'asylum', he finally took the step of saying goodbye to his country of birth. And that was the beginning of the new Korchnoi.

If the Russians had been preparing to pension off their old warrior, he proved that any such plans for his retirement would have been premature. In the next year, his results in the Candidates matches were better than anything he had accomplished earlier in his career. Fortune's quirky sense of humour had ensured that all Korchnoi's matches would be against Soviet opponents. Their task was made no easier by the reaction of the Soviet authorities to Korchnoi's defection. He was immediately branded a traitor and all Soviet grandmasters were invited to sign a statement in condemnation of his act of treason. He was also the subject of a boycott in international tournaments. Although this was never official policy, no Soviet or other Eastern European players would participate in any event to which Korchnoi had been involved. When accused of operating a boycott, the Soviet Chess Federation explained that this behaviour was an individual decision on the part of each player who refused to compete against the traitor. There had even been an attempt to have Korchnoi excluded from the 1977 Candidates series, but the International Chess Federation refused to comply with the Soviet request.

By the time the first round of the Candidates started, relations between Korchnoi and the Soviet Chess Federation were soured beyond hope of any reconciliation. Worse still, Korchnoi had again been paired against his old enemy Tigran Petrosian. The match was played in an atmosphere of unprecedented tension and bitterness. Handshakes, common courtesies and even any form of conversation between the players were abandoned, and that set the tone for all future matches between Korchnoi and his former compatriots. After beating Petrosian, Korchnoi moved on to destroy Polugayevsky, for whom the stresses were simply too great. In the final he defeated Boris Spassky to secure his second chance of a match with Karpov.

The happenings in Baguio City are already part of chess history. An interesting feature of the aftermath of the match was the behaviour of the contestants when it was all over. Karpov rested from tournament play for several months, but all Korchnoi wanted to do was to play chess. He flew directly to the Chess Olympics in Buenos Aires and proceeded to play for Switzerland, his adopted country, right through the event. He looked tired and was clearly not on his best form, but still made the best score on first board.

By qualifying for yet another match against Karpov, Korchnoi has extended the period of World Championship domination by these two great players. Since Fischer stopped playing in 1972 there have been only two names in the contest for the title. Korchnoi's play in the year before the present match was not as impressive as in 1977, but he has overcome all opposition once again. Whatever one may think of his vitriolic temperament, in purely chess terms, his is a remarkable achievement of longevity.

Korchnoi's chess style is not easy to characterize. Perhaps the sheer depth and complexity of his strategic ideas are the outstanding features. In 1958, writing in their book *The Soviet School of Chess*, Kotov and Yudovich wrote: 'Original plans, a constant quest for the new, good combinational vision, and a high level of technique are the features of Korchnoi's playing. Sometimes he takes unnecessary risks, underestimates his opponent's defensive resources, and builds too elaborate formations – but all these are growing pains.' Most of those words remain true, so perhaps we must deduce that Korchnoi has never properly grown up. In one respect, however, that description no longer fits. Korchnoi has long been regarded as a supreme defensive player, and one who, far from underestimating his opponents' resources, tends to regard any position as defensible unless proved otherwise. His attacking style is cumbersome (likened once to a cripple lurching forward swinging his crutches), but his counterattacks come swiftly and decisively.

Korchnoi is a perfectionist in his play, always willing to spend time looking for the very best moves, until pressure of the clock forces him to rush. He used to revel in time-shortage, and remains very impressive even when only seconds remain on his clock. He has apparently mastered the art of thinking in his opponent's time and seeing just a little further than they do. In recent years he has shown a sensible fear of extreme time-trouble, but will still occasionally leave himself with only a minute or two for a dozen moves. In such circumstances anything can happen, but more often than not it is Korchnoi's opponent who becomes flustered and makes the decisive error.

A particularly impressive feature of Korchnoi's play is his ability to hold together ragged-looking positions and weave deep designs around their constituent parts. His game against Ivkov from the 1967 USSR–Yugoslavia match is a fine example of such chessboard tapestry:

White: V. Korchnoi   Black: B. Ivkov

1 P–Q4 P–Q4 2 P–QB4 P–K3 3 N–QB3 B–K2 4 P×P P×P 5 B–B4 P–QB3 6 P–K3 B–KB4 7 P–KN4 B–K3 8 P–KR3 P–KR4 9 P×P!

(White's extra pawn looks meaningless and too feeble to survive, but watch how Korchnoi builds his whole strategy round it) 9 . . . N–Q2 10 R–R2! QN–B3 11 B–K2 B–Q3 12 B×B Q×B 13 R–N2 K–B1 14 B–N4 N–R3 15 Q–B3 Q–Q2 16 B×B Q×B 17 KN–K2 Q–B4 18 N–B4 Q–B7 19 Q–K2 Q×Q+ 20 K×Q N–B4 21 R–N5 *(Still the pawn on R5 lives, and as long as it remains on the board, the black rooks will remain uncoordinated)* 21 . . . N–Q3 22 QR–KN1 N(Q3)–K1 23 P–B3 R–Q1 24 K–Q3 R–R3 25 QN–K2 R–Q2 26 P–N3 R–K2 27 N–N3 N–Q3 28 N–B5 N×N 29 R×N K–N1 30 R(5)–N5 R–R2

31 P–N4! *(Finally the minority attack starts. White advances a pawn to QN5 in order to provoke weaknesses in the black Q-side. This is the standard plan after White's pawn exchange at move four, but Korchnoi's creative opening and middlegame play have made it all the more powerful with Black's rook out of play on KR2)* 31 . . . P–R3 32 P–QR4 K–B1 33 P–N5 RP×P 34 P×P N–K1 35 R–N1 N–Q3 36 P×P P×P 37 R–QB1 *(Delicately timed, waiting for the black knight move so that he no longer has R–R3 as a defence)* 37 . . . N–B5 38 P–K4 *(Finally the advance of the centre pawn which is another characteristic plan in this Queen's Gambit exchange variation)* 38 . . . N–N7+ 39 K–B3 N–R5+ 40 K–N4 P×P *(Desperation, but 40 . . . N–N3 41 R×BP wins easily for White)* 41 K×N P×P 42 R–KB5! R–K5 43 K–N3 R–R3 *(The QP was immune thanks to N–K6+)* 44 K–B3 R–Q3 45 R–QR1! *(Threatening a mating attack with N–N6+)* 45 . . . R–K6+ 46 K–B4 K–N1 47 R–R8+ K–R2 48 R×P R–B3 49 R(7)–B8 R×R 50 R×R R–K1 *(A last trick; if 51 R×R? P–B7!)* 51 R–B5 resigns. Not a spectacular game, but a good example of Korchnoi's skill in building 'elaborate formations' and making them work.

Chess in the USSR

Why are the Russians (or to be accurate the Soviets) so good at chess? Despite Korchnoi's vehemently expressed political views, we must remember that both players in this match were born in the Soviet Union and learnt their chess there. Indeed, with the single exception of the American Bobby Fischer, every contestant in a World Championship match since the war has been a Soviet citizen. So what makes them so good? The answer to that question must be found in the roots of Soviet culture and the highly respected place given to the game of chess and its leading practitioners in that culture.

Even in pre-revolutionary Russia, there had been a strong chess tradition. There were great tournaments in St Petersburg in 1909 and 1914, and Mikhail Tchigorin (1850–1908) had been a leading player of his day and a challenger for the world title. The game of chess was held in high regard by both Marx and Lenin, but until the revolution was largely a leisure activity of the privileged classes. The 'Glorious October' of 1917 changed all that. From the earliest days of Lenin's power, chess had its role to play in the promised democratization of society and the provision of leisure and cultural pursuits for the masses. That role became ever more important until chess was firmly established as part of the daily Soviet cultural life.

Two men stand out in the history of Soviet chess for their parts in establishing the game so firmly in the country. Both were high government officials with a passionate interest in chess. A. F. Ilyin-Zhenevsky (1894–1941) was one of the leading chessmasters, who also happened to hold the post of Chief Commissar at the headquarters of the General Reservists Organization in Moscow. He had a genuine love of chess and a missionary zeal to spread the game throughout his vast land. In this task, he had the powerful support of N. V. Krylenko, a leading political figure with a fanatical dedication to the cause of chess in the Soviet Union.

Ilyin-Zhenevsky was the thinker of the pair. He realized that the revolution gave opportunities to build on the Russian chess tradition. The principal responsibility of his Commissar's job was to provide physical and military training for reservists prior to their conscription into the Red Army. Sport had been included in the curriculum for its influence on a man's character rather than just for physical well-being. Seizing on that fact, Ilyin-Zhenevsky was able to extol the virtues of chess as a means of learning disciplined thought, persistence and caution; not only that, but chess would teach the elements of strategy to future military men.

Besides organizing chess for the military, Ilyin-Zhenevsky worked hard to set up national chess organizations, to run tournaments and encourage the growth of the game. Between 1920 and 1924 an argument raged concerning the place of chess in the new society. A one-day conference was held in 1920 to discuss the question. Were the chess-players to be encouraged simply to get on with the game on their own, or was chess too important to escape from state control? Ilyin-Zhenevksy's firm belief, which eventually won the day, was that chess must become an integral part of the new socialist culture. Chess had a right to exist only if it were popularized among the masses. 'In this country, where the workers have gained victory, chess cannot be apolitical as in capitalist countries.'

By 1924, the idea that chess had a role to play in the formation of an ideal socialist society had taken firm root. The official view, stated at a conference in Moscow that year, proclaimed: 'Chess is a political weapon which must be used . . . to give to the working masses, tired after their daily labour, a rational leisure activity.' In the same year, a national chess magazine was founded and chess tournaments sprang up everywhere. There were city championships, workers' tournaments and championships of the Red Army and Navy.

The editor of the chess magazine (called '64') was N. V. Krylenko. He had been Commissar for War in the first Bolshevik government, became Commander-in-chief of the Russian forces after the revolution and had been public prosecutor for the revolutionary tribunals in 1918. In 1936 he was to become Commissar of Justice for the USSR. Not a bad pedigree for a chess magazine editor. He must have been a very busy man for, besides his editorship, he wrote a great deal and was also head of the chess section of the Supreme Council for Physical Culture. Later he took on the mantle of General Secretary of the Soviet Chess Federation. Krylenko was the man of action, the Lenin to Ilyin-Zhenevsky's Marx. His statements on plans for the advancement of Soviet chess became progressively more fanatical as his career developed. In 1925 his attitude seemed highly perceptive and realistic: 'In our country where the cultural level is comparatively low, where up to now a typical pastime of the masses has been brewing liquor, drunkenness and brawling, chess is a powerful means of raising the general cultural level.' By 1932, he was taking a more militant stand: 'We must finish once and for all with the neutrality of chess. We must condemn once and for all the formula "chess for the sake of chess", like the formula "art for art's sake". We must organize shock-brigades of chessplayers and begin the immediate realization of a Five-Year Plan for chess.'

There is no doubt that Krylenko played a crucial part in the development of Soviet chess in the period between the wars, so it was rather ungrateful of Stalin to have him shot in 1938. One of the charges against Krylenko was: 'retarding the development of chess and cutting it off from the social and political life of the nation.' One of the Great Leader's little jokes, I think.

In the early years after the revolution, Soviet chess organization was primarily concerned with development of the game within its own national boundaries. As the country settled down, there grew an increasing preoccupation with the question of the role of chess in an international context. In 1924 the International Chess Federation (FIDE) had been founded and the Soviet Chess Section was invited to join. The reply was unequivocal: 'The Executive Committee of the Soviet Chess Section declared that Russian Chess Organizations were not only not neutral politically, but indeed stood quite firmly on the platform of class warfare and the international working-class movement; consequently it was quite impossible for them to enter an international organization which did not share that platform.'

In many similar statements of this period, one senses the hand of Ilyin-Zhenevsky, paying strong lip-service to the creed of international socialism, in which he no doubt believed, while also doing all he could to further the cause of chess itself, in which perhaps he believed even more fervently: chess can be of service to the Cause, but our noble game will also benefit from government support. And the benefits were huge, with virtually unlimited funds available to finance the formation of chess clubs and organized tournaments. The ambivalent attitude comes through very strongly in statements concerning the great tournament of Moscow 1925 (in which Ilyin-Zhenevsky himself performed creditably). A strong tournament would be of great benefit to Soviet chess, but how could one justify sending invitations to the professional masters of the West? The solution was a masterpiece of dialectical rationalization: '. . . in certain conditions the participation of working-class chessplayers in bourgeois tournaments would be politically advantageous, inasmuch as it would unite the workers around the idea of class solidarity and of their opposition, as a class, to the bourgeoisie . . . in order through victories over bourgeois masters to increase among the proletarian masses self-respect and faith in their strength.' A sort of 'Let's all gang up against Capablanca' philosophy.

By the late 1920s chess was really taking hold among the Soviet workers. The numbers of registered players had risen from 1000 in 1923 to 24,000 in 1924, and by 1929 the figure was 150,000. Numbers have continued to rise ever since, with the half-million mark passed in 1934, a million in 1951, and the latest estimate is four and a half million.

Even with the support of such influential figures as Krylenko and Ilyin-Zhenevsky, the astonishing popularity of the game deserves some further explanation. Financial support and the sheer passion of the organizers were a great help, of course (and in chess a little money can go a long way), but, above all, the highly respected image of the chessmaster must have been responsible for attracting large numbers to the game. The qualities needed to succeed at chess were supposed to be almost identical to those desired of the model communist. This put the chessplayer on a pedestal above the imperfection of ordinary men. The nation had to learn chess as a path to self-government. As one article in *Pravda* explained: 'Our great teachers, Marx and Lenin, devoted themselves enthusiastically to chess in their leisure hours. They saw in it primarily a means of strengthening the will, a training ground for resolve and nervous energy. Lenin's chief interest in chess lay in the stubborn struggle . . . and in finding the way out of a difficult, sometimes almost hopeless situation.'

There seem to be no games of Lenin extant, but the April 1970 issue of *Shakhmaty v SSSR* celebrates the centenary of his birth with an article including some chess problems he is known to have solved.

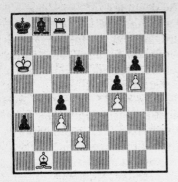

This position was composed by the 'well-known Marxist revolutionary' P. N. Lepeshinsky. White to move and mate in three moves. Without moving the pieces, Lenin found the solution in five minutes. The answer is given at the end of this chapter.

On the theme of great teachers, Stalin deserves a brief mention also. His chess achievements do not appear to have been great, but there is one game reputedly won by Stalin against his good friend the head of the secret police in 1926:

White: Stalin   Black: Yezhov

1 P–K4 P–QB4 2 N–KB3 P–Q3 3 P–Q4 P×P 4 N×P N–KB3
5 N–QB3 QN–Q2 6 B–K2 P–QR3 7 0–0 P–K3 8 P–B4 P–QN4
9 P–QR3 B–N2 10 B–B3 Q–N3 11 B–K3 Q–B2 12 Q–K2 B–K2
13 P–KN4 N–B4 14 Q–N2 0–0 15 QR–Q1 KR–K1 16 P–N5 KN–Q2
17 R–Q2 P–K4 18 N–B5 N–K3 19 N×B+ R×N 20 P–B5 N–Q5
21 P–B6 KR–K1 22 B–R5 P–N3 23 B×P! RP×B 24 Q–R3 N–K3
25 Q–R6 Q–Q1 26 R–B3 N×BP 27 P×N R–QB1 28 R(Q2)–B2
Q×P (*There is no other defence to 29 R–R3*) 29 R×Q and White won.

Lenin died in 1924 and after Stalin had won the fight to succeed him the great chess movement began to take another direction. On the home front, Stalin introduced his first Five-Year Plan in 1928. The primary goal was to overtake the most advanced countries of the capitalist West. Chessplayers were expected to play an important part in reaching this goal. 'The present widespread interest in chess and chess tournaments must be transformed into competitions to raise productivity,' and 'The chess organization has every right to demand that chessplayers should be in the front ranks of the fighters for the building of socialism,' were typical of the pronouncements of that time to exhort chessplayers to give their best efforts to the great cause. But on the whole the chessplayers just wanted to play chess.

Meanwhile, there was much criticism of the Western way of chess and self-congratulation for the way the game was organized in the

USSR. Rokhlin in 1929 wrote of 'the degrading of chess under the corrupt influence of the Western European bourgeois café', and Ilyin-Zhenevsky in 1931 described Western chess in the following terms: '. . . the centres of chess life in most bourgeois countries are first-class cafés . . . a working man, if he were poorly dressed, would simply not be let in.' He went on to complain about the prices, too.

All this time, both numbers and the strength of Soviet players were growing. Chess was one of the few seedlings planted after the revolution which had borne fruit. It therefore became ever more important as an example of the success of the aims of the revolution. Chess was already far more than a mere game. The Soviet historian M. S. Kogan wrote in 1931: 'From the point of view of the revolutionary vanguard of the proletariat, chess is not an end in itself but a means of raising the cultural (and thereby also the political) level of the labouring masses of the world.' But success at chess did come close to being an end in itself, with the individual World Championship very high on the list of priorities.

In 1927, Alekhine had beaten Capablanca for the title. This left ambivalent attitudes within the USSR. On the one hand, Alekhine was a Soviet citizen and winner of the first Russian championship in 1920, but he had left the USSR in 1921 to seek fame in Paris. When he had achieved his aim, there was hope that he would return to the country of his birth and lead Soviet chess to further glories. In a speech at an emigré's dinner given in his honour in Paris, Alekhine made his feelings all too clear by expressing his hopes 'that the country will soon be liberated from the Bolshevik yoke'. As Ilyin-Zhenevsky sadly admitted: 'This speech finally severs Alekhine's ties with the Soviet chess community and places him in the ranks of our irreconcilable enemies.' But when it was suggested that Alekhine's games should no longer be published in the Soviet Union, Ilyin-Zhenevsky the chess-player reasserted himself: 'Whatever Alekhine may be from a political point of view, he continues to be the strongest present-day player. Our study of the art of chess will be incomplete if we ignore Alekhine.' Thirty years later, Alekhine was, in fact, completely rehabilitated and is now viewed officially as the second great Russian player (after Tchigorin). The quality of his games appears to transcend the minor aberration of leaving his homeland and denouncing its new rulers.

It is a matter for speculation whether one day Korchnoi, too, will resume his place on the Soviet list of honour. Alekhine, after all, learnt his chess under the tyranny of the Tsars; his credentials for being a great Soviet player appear considerably less convincing than those of Korchnoi, but that will be a matter for future re-writers of Soviet history to decide.

The first truly great player to emerge from the post-revolutionary chess movement was Mikhail Botvinnik. He was the dominating figure in Soviet chess for almost thirty years from 1930, and was the first Soviet player to gain considerable international success. In the Moscow International Tournament of 1935, he shared first place ahead of many of the finest players in the world. At Nottingham 1936 he tied for first place with Capablanca and put Soviet chess firmly on the map. After that success a telegram was sent to Stalin from one of the Soviet delegation at the tournament, but in Botvinnik's name:

Dear beloved teacher and leader . . . My ardent desire to uphold the honour of Soviet chess made me put into my play all my strength, knowledge and energy . . . I am infinitely happy to be able to report that a representative of Soviet chess has shared first place in the tournament with ex-champion of the world Capablanca. This was only possible because I sensed behind me the support of my whole country, the care of our government and our party and above all that daily care which you, our great leader, have taken and still take, to raise to unprecedented heights our great motherland and to rear in us representatives of Soviet youth a healthy and joyful generation in all fields of our socialist construction. Inspired by your slogan 'catch up and surpass', I am glad that I have been able to realize it, if only on that small sector on which our country has entrusted me to fight.

A no less sickening article appeared in *Pravda* on the day of Botvinnik's victory, explaining how he was helped by sensing 'the powerful breathing of his great motherland'. This began a new and more confident phase in the development of Soviet chess. In Botvinnik they knew they had a man who could win the World Championship, and there were others of his generation not far behind him.

During the years of the Second World War, chess tournaments continued to be organized in the USSR, despite the difficulties, and their young players developed their talents rapidly while the rest of the world slipped far behind. By the time the war was over, the USSR was ready to dominate the world of chess.

Stalin's deputy, A. Zhdanov, had stressed the importance of culture in waging battle against the bourgeoisie. Chess was to be one of the spearheads of the cultural offensive. At least this attitude encouraged a more outward-looking approach, and the USSR finally joined FIDE in 1947. This was their first venture into international competition, apart from a brief flirtation with an organization called Workers Chess International which had a strife-ridden existence between 1926 and 1931, finally torn apart by internal battles between socialists and communists.

The main aim was still to win the World Championship, but Alekhine's death in 1946 had left the throne vacant. FIDE organized a match tournament to be contested among the six leading players of the time. When Reuben Fine declined to participate, the number was reduced to five. The result was a total success for the Soviet players: Botvinnik won by a handsome margin, Smyslov was second, Keres and Reshevsky shared third, and Euwe, the only living ex-champion, lagged behind. So only the American grandmaster, Reshevsky, could still hope to live with the Russians in tournament play. Paul Keres, of course, had joined the ranks of Soviet grandmasters when Stalin had annexed Estonia. Botvinnik's published comments on his great victory continued to extol the virtues of the system: 'It is a victory of Soviet patriots, educated and cared for by our great party of Lenin and Stalin. We shall fight for new successes of Soviet culture to the glory of our beloved motherland.' Later he wrote: 'The historic contest between Soviet and capitalist chess has ended in a complete victory for the Soviet school of chess.' This line continued until the death of Stalin. 'Every new international victory of our sportsmen is a victory for the Soviet regime and the socialist system of physical education; it provides indisputable proof of the superiority of socialist culture over the declining culture of capitalist countries,' wrote Kotov and Yudovich in their 1951 work, *The Soviet School of Chess*, 'Bourgeois sport enflames low passions and cripples men spiritually and physically. It is ruled by the laws of private enterprise and the profit motive.'

After Stalin came a distinct thaw. By the mid-1950s there was nobody to challenge the Soviet stranglehold on the World Championship. Botvinnik, Bronstein, Smyslov, Keres and Boleslavsky were the five best players in the world. While still allowing heavy propaganda to appear under his name, Botvinnik worked hard for the cause of chess. His was the principal hand behind the rehabilitation of Alekhine, a man whose political crimes could evidently be forgiven because of the excellence of his chess. There was also a general change in official attitudes towards the presentation of international sport to promote peace and goodwill.

During the Krushchev years, Soviet chessplayers competed more and more in tournaments outside their own country. Rarely did they fail to capture the first prize. The first challenge to their supremacy came only in the mid-1960s, when the Danish grandmaster Bent Larsen and the American Bobby Fischer began regularly taking top places ahead of the Soviet representatives. In 1970 a match was played in Belgrade between teams representing the USSR and the Rest of the World. Ten years before, such an encounter would have been an overwhelming victory for the Soviet team, but in Belgrade they only scraped home by a single point. While still impressive that a single land could defeat the combined forces of the opposition, the result marked the beginning of a depressing phase for Soviet chess hegemony. Two years later, they lost the World Championship to Fischer.

The leading Soviet players fell under heavy criticism. They had been enjoying their carefree tournament life too much and had neglected their duties both to the game and to the state. Steps were taken immediately to intensify the competition for international invitations and to ensure a return to the competitive attitudes which had won the title in Botvinnik's time. The older players, Spassky, Smyslov, Petrosian, Tal and Korchnoi, had been guilty of letting their standards fall. They were in disgrace and were forced again to compete in Soviet Championships in order to re-establish their credentials.

Then along came Karpov, the answer to the prayers (if such are permitted) of the Soviet Chess Federation. Giving their young super-star every possible support, they carried him to the World Championship and brought the title back to Moscow after the shortest possible absence, only three years.

That was the chess atmosphere under which Korchnoi had grown up. A country with a proud chess tradition, inextricably linked to the political system, a land where, for example, a chess tournament for collective farm workers in the winter of 1949 had attracted an entry of 130,000, where chess was part of the way of life and one of the acclaimed successes of the system. To turn his back on all that and, worse still, to proceed to attack the Soviet establishment, were unforgiveable acts. Korchnoi's treason could not go unpunished.

For a year after his defection, the name of Viktor Korchnoi ceased to appear in Soviet chess magazines. But it was hard to pretend for long that he did not exist, so verbal attacks on him began to appear as a prelude to the inclusion of his name in chess reports. Perhaps the chess reports of the 1977 Candidates matches had looked too odd, with strange mentions of events in which only one player appeared to be participating. Similar treatment had been meted out to Ludek Pachman, the Czechoslovakian grandmaster who had dared to oppose the Soviet intervention in his country in 1968. Both Pachman and Korchnoi have since been boycotted by players from Warsaw pact countries in invitation events.

The motto of FIDE is *Gens una sumus*, we are one people, but for the Soviet chess establishment, that creed of friendship cannot be stretched to embrace a non-person such as Viktor Korchnoi.

Lenin's mate in three: 1 B–R2 P–Q4 2 P–Q4 P×P e.p. 3 B×P mate; not too difficult for the Great Theorist.

The World Chess Championship

For the first twelve centuries or so of its existence, the game of chess managed to survive very well without a World Championship. The earliest references to chess, or a very similar game, are found in Indian poetry of the seventh century, so we assume that is where chess originated. The rules at that time led to a much slower game, with the powers of many pieces weaker than in the modern game. The queen, for example, was only permitted to move diagonally, and only one square at a time. Only when the game reached Europe in the sixteenth century were the rules changed to suit the Western temperament.

There is little record of serious chess competition before the nineteenth century, and only in the second half of that century did tournament play begin. Until then, France had long been the centre of European chess, having boasted the great masters Danican-Philidor (1726–95) and La Bourdonnais (1797–1840), both of whom were without doubt the finest players of their time. In 1843, the English master and Shakespearian scholar, Howard Staunton, defeated the Frenchman, Saint-Amant, to take the unofficial title across the channel. In 1851, Staunton himself was the instigator of the first great international tournament. Held in London to coincide with the Great Exhibition, it took the form of a series of knock-out matches between the best players from all over Europe. The winner was the German, Adolf Anderssen.

The next great nineteenth-century player was Paul Morphy, an American who, in 1858, travelled to Europe and won matches against all the leading Europeans, including Anderssen, with some ease. Staunton claimed pressure of work and avoided meeting the American. Morphy returned to America and practically gave up chess. This left a strange situation; chess was entering a competitive era which demanded a World Champion, but the best player would not play. Only Morphy's death in 1884 left the way free to organize an official match for the World Championship. The two strongest players of the day were Wilhelm Steinitz, who had succeeded Anderssen as Germany's best, and Johannes Zukertort, a man of many talents and greater boasts, who had won the tournament of London 1883 three points ahead of Steinitz.

The match was played in the United States in 1886. Zukertort raced to a 4-1 lead, but Steinitz gradually overhauled him. The final result was a 12½-7½ victory to Steinitz, who thus became the first official World Champion. He successfully fought off challenges to his title from the Russian Mikhail Tchigorin (in two separate matches in 1889 and 1892) and from Gunsberg in 1890.

But Steinitz was already fifty years old when he won the title; soon he had to give way to a younger man. The successful challenge came from Emanuel Lasker in 1894 by the convincing score of 12-7. Two years later Steinitz made the mistake of playing a return match which he lost by the disastrous margin of 12½-4½. Lasker was to remain champion for more than a quarter of a century. Marshall, Tarrasch and Janowski all made unsuccessful challenges. The nearest Lasker came to being deposed was against Schlechter in 1910, when a short match of ten games was drawn, with Lasker scoring the equalizing victory only in the final game.

Next in the roll of honour came the great Cuban, Jose Raul Capablanca. When the challenge came in 1921, Lasker was fifty-three years old and disinclined to fight. He would have been happy to give up his title, but the public demanded a match. Of the first nine games, eight were drawn and Capablanca won the other. Then Lasker weakened badly, scoring only two draws from the next five games. With the score at 9-5 to the Cuban, Lasker resigned the match and his title.

Capablanca had already acquired a reputation for invincibility. His style was quiet and positional, with a phenomenal technique. His losses were exceedingly rare and always made news. So it was surprising when he lost the title the first time he was called upon to defend it, in 1927 against Alexander Alekhine. Their match was a bitter affair between two men who despised each other (though most of the venom emanated from Alekhine). It was also the dullest match in World Championship history, with only nine decisive games from thirty-four contested. Alekhine scored six wins to Capablanca's three, and the unbeatable Cuban had been deposed.

Ever since the first World Championship match in 1886, there had been no official organization to arrange such matches and decide who had the right to challenge the title-holder. Despite the formation of

FIDE (International Chess Federation) in 1924, this remained the state of affairs, with the title being at the personal disposal of its owner, to defend when he pleased against whom he pleased. Only the pressures of public opinion and the lure of money were present to ensure that the champion did indeed meet his best qualified opponents. This had not worked badly, though on one or two occasions very strong players were denied title matches for want of a rich backer. The Lasker–Capablanca match had needed a purse of $20,000 to lure the defending champion to play. Capablanca too had made it difficult for Alekhine to raise sufficient funds to satisfy his demands.

With the title firmly in his grasp, Alekhine decided to make it still more difficult for Capablanca to secure a return match. They talked a great deal, but never agreed terms. In the meantime, Alekhine played two leisurely defences of his title against Bogolyubov (in 1929 and 1934), a strong grandmaster, but not quite in the class of Capablanca. What was surely intended to be another easy defence came badly unstuck when Alekhine met Dr Max Euwe, a Dutchman renowned for his vast theoretical knowledge and intense preparation. In bad physical and mental shape, Alekhine lost a close match 15½-14½ to give Euwe the title in 1935. The magnanimous victor readily agreed to a return encounter. Alekhine prepared properly and two years later regained his title by the convincing score of 15½-9½.

By now there was a host of younger grandmasters queueing up for a crack at the title. Botvinnik, Keres, Flohr and Fine all had strong claims to be the next challenger, but the war put an end to the confusion.

In 1946, after agreeing to defend his title against Botvinnik, Alekhine died suddenly. FIDE at last took the opportunity to introduce a fair system by which to run the World Championship. A match-tournament would be held for the vacant title and thereafter the holder would be required to defend his title every three years. The challenger each time would be determined by a series of eliminating tournaments. And so were born the Zonal, Interzonal and Candidates tournaments, the leading players at each stage qualifying for the next stage, until only eight candidates were left. They would then do battle for the right to challenge the champion.

Mikhail Botvinnik won the 1948 match-tournament to gain Alekhine's bequest, and to begin an era of astonishing domination of the title by Soviet players. The first to emerge as challenger was David Bronstein in 1951. Botvinnik survived narrowly to draw the match

12-12, despite having been one down with two to play. The rules specified a twenty-four game match, with the champion retaining his title in the case of a draw, so Botvinnik was safe for another three years. In 1954 he drew another match, this time with Smyslov, but in 1957 had to concede victory to the same opponent by $12\frac{1}{2}$-$9\frac{1}{2}$.

Vassily Smyslov was World Chess Champion for only one year. The rules of FIDE gave a defeated champion the right to a return match the following year. Botvinnik studied his opponent more thoroughly this time and regained his title by a score of $12\frac{1}{2}$-$10\frac{1}{2}$.

The programme was repeated on the next occasion, only this time the great Latvian Mikhail Tal took Smyslov's part. Tal beat Botvinnik convincingly in 1960, only to be crushed the following year by an amazingly energetic and youthful fifty-year-old. The USSR was doing a fine job in stockpiling ex-World Champions. For a long time, only Euwe had held that august title. Now he had been joined by Smyslov and Tal. The general congress of FIDE began to think that Botvinnik was making too great a use of the return match clause, so they abolished it. To show his disapproval, Botvinnik lost his next match to Tigran Petrosian, who thus, in 1963, became the ninth World Chess Champion.

We were then treated to an era of Petrosian–Spassky matches, just as Botvinnik and Smyslov had dominated the scene a decade before. In 1966, the Armenian champion survived Spassky's challenge to win by $12\frac{1}{2}$-$11\frac{1}{2}$, but three years later Spassky was happy to relieve his opponent of the title by a score of $12\frac{1}{2}$-$10\frac{1}{2}$.

Boris Spassky must have been the unluckiest of the World Champions. Unlucky to be the man in possession when Bobby Fischer decided to seize the title. Fischer was perhaps the greatest player in the modern history of the game; he was also the most difficult. His frequent withdrawals from tournaments, and total withdrawals from competitive play for long periods, slowed down his career considerably. But when he finally consented to play through a qualifying series for the World Championship he was unstoppable. His easy win in the Interzonal tournament was followed by unprecedented 6-0 victories against Taimanov and Larsen in Candidates matches, followed by a $6\frac{1}{2}$-$2\frac{1}{2}$ win against Petrosian. After that, many considered that Spassky did well to hold Fischer to $12\frac{1}{2}$-$8\frac{1}{2}$ (though it must be admitted that one of Spassky's points was won by default).

So Bobby Fischer was World Champion, but those games against Spassky were the last he has played. In 1975, when the time came for him to defend his title against Anatoly Karpov, he submitted a huge list of more than a hundred additions and changes to the rules: if they were not made, he would not play. FIDE conceded all his demands except two. Fischer refused the match. FIDE conceded one of the remaining two points, thinking that a reasonable compromise. But with Fischer there is no compromise. In 1975, Anatoly Karpov became the twelfth Chess Champion of the World, and the first to gain the title by default.

Thus we entered the Karpov–Korchnoi era. Just as Botvinnik and Smyslov had dominated the matches in the 1950s, and Petrosian and Spassky the 1960s, the last decade has seen only the two Ks. Will Korchnoi join the band of forgotten men who have challenged unsuccessfully, or can he become World Champion number thirteen? As David Bronstein once sadly remarked, you can only be World Champion for a few years, but you remain an ex-World Champion for the rest of your life. Korchnoi would dearly love the temporary honour of the title as well as the lasting fame it would confer on his name. And there is nobody from whom he would prefer to wrench the crown than Anatoly Karpov.

Close Encounters

When Korchnoi and Karpov began their first match in 1974 honours were even between them, each having won two of the five tournament games previously contested. They had also finished level in a short training match played in 1971, though that was a somewhat unnatural encounter with Karpov having white in every game, but Korchnoi choosing what openings were to be played. By 1974 there was already a strong personal antipathy between the two grandmasters. Korchnoi was one of the older generation, discredited in the eyes of the Soviet Chess Federation by the exploits of Bobby Fischer. Karpov was the great white hope, destined to recapture the World Championship. The might of Soviet chess organization was behind him in his quest. Korchnoi's own attitude towards Karpov was less enthusiastic: the youth was more confident than he had any right to be, and as a chessplayer still had much to learn from his elders.

So the match started in Moscow with emotions strained. Not only were Karpov and Korchnoi hardly on speaking terms, but the state had almost been reached where no friend of Karpov would be seen talking to a friend of Korchnoi. Karpov's great success in the semi-final against Spassky had made him a clear favourite, so Korchnoi was fighting against form, predictions, the Soviet Chess Federation and the plans of destiny. The match was scheduled for a maximum of twenty-four games, but if either player scored five wins before that time, he would be declared the winner.

Within six games, Karpov had taken a 2-0 lead, with two incisive victories with the white pieces. The first of these was a particularly impressive piece of opening preparation.

White: Karpov   Black: Korchnoi
Sicilian Defence

1 P–K4 P–QB4 2 N–KB3 P–Q3 3 P–Q4 P×P 4 N×P N–KB3 5 N–QB3 P–KN3 (*The dragon variation is an old love of Korchnoi, though*

after this game he was not to play it again) 6 B–K3 B–N2 7 P–B3 N–B3 8 Q–Q2 0–0 9 B–QB4 B–Q2 10 P–KR4 R–B1 11 B–N3 N–K4 12 0–0–0 N–B5 (*As usual in this variation, the game develops into a race between the attacks on opposite wings. White's attack is easier to play, because it is simpler to open lines on the K-side thanks to Black's advanced KN-pawn.*) 13 B×N R×B 14 P–R5 N×RP 15 P–KN4 N–B3 16 N(Q4)–K2 (*For his sacrificed pawn, White has opened the KR-file and gained time for his assault on the black king. First he supports the knight on QB3, while preparing to bring its colleague to KN3 or KB4*) 16 . . . Q–R4 (*Later games showed that 16 . . . R–K1 was better*) 17 B–R6 B×B 18 Q×B KR–B1 19 R–Q3! R(B5)–B4

20 P–N5! R×P 21 R–Q5! (*Having lured the rook to the K-side, White now ensures that his knight reaches Q5 and eliminates the crucial black defender on KB3*) 21 . . . R×R 22 N×R R–K1 23 N(K2)–B4 B–B3 24 P–K5! B×N (*24 . . . P×P 25 N×N+ P×N 26 N–R5! P×N 27 R–N1+ forces mate. The point of 24 P–K5! was to eliminate the defence of 26 . . . Q–N4+ in this line*) 25 P×N P×P 26 Q×RP+ K–B1 27 Q–R8+ resigns (*27 . . . K–K2 28 N×B+ Q×N 29 R–K1+ would be the finish*).

After this early spurt by Karpov, many expected the match to be over rapidly, but Korchnoi settled down and the next ten games were all drawn. During this period of the match, Korchnoi had no trouble holding his games with black. He played the French Defence throughout and never looked in danger. With the white pieces he was pushing hard, but never quite breaking through. Nevertheless, Korchnoi was optimistic. At this stage of the match he was heard to remark to the American chess journalist, Grandmaster Robert Byrne, 'I've got him now, he's playing like . . . ', Korchnoi groped for the appropriate simile, ' . . . like a wet dish-rag!'.

In the seventeenth game, however, all Korchnoi's hopes faded. He had Karpov under considerable pressure throughout the game, but blundered in time-trouble to throw everything away. He lost that game, and the score was 3-0 to Karpov with only seven games left to play. Another draw followed and the match seemed set to drift peacefully to an end. Then, unbelievably, Korchnoi started to fight back. He scored his first win in the nineteenth game, grinding out the full point from a long ending. In game twenty-one, something much more surprising happened. Karpov lost in nineteen moves.

White: Korchnoi   Black: Karpov
Queen's Indian Defence

1 P–Q4 N–KB3 2 N–KB3 P–K3 3 P–KN3 P–QN3 4 B–N2 B–N2 5 P–B4 B–K2 6 N–B3 0–0 7 Q–B2 P–B4 8 P–Q5 P×P 9 N–KN5 N–B3 10 N×QP P–N3 11 Q–Q2! (*A surprising, but highly effective way to take advantage of the weak squares round Black's king*) 11 . . . N×N? (*A mistake which prepares a blunder*) 12 B×N R–N1?

13 N×RP! R–K1 (*13 . . . K×N would have lost to 14 Q–R6+ K–N1   15 Q×P+ K–R1   16 Q–R6+ K–N1 17 B–K4 P–B4 18 B–Q5+ R–B2 19 Q–N6+*) 14 Q–R6 N–K4 (*Black could easily have resigned here; he is soon forced to surrender more material to avoid mate*) 15 N–N5 B×N 16 B×KB Q×B   (*Otherwise B–B6 and Q–R8 mate*) 17 Q×Q B×B   18 0–0 B×P 19 P–B4 resigns.

Suddenly the match had become quite dramatic. Korchnoi had three games remaining in which to score the win needed to equalize. And Karpov looked very tired indeed. Korchnoi was too exhausted himself and made no further impression. The last three games were tamely drawn and Karpov took the match by three wins to two with nineteen draws.

So to Baguio City, where the stakes were much higher. Not only was there a prize fund of a quarter of a million pounds, but the match was officially for the World Championship. In Moscow they had only been playing for the right to challenge Fischer. Also, of course, Korchnoi was now an official enemy of the Soviet people and the politics had become international. The match in the Philippines will long be remembered more for its off-the-board incidents than for the games, though there was no shortage of good chess. Gurus, parapsychologists, mirror glasses and yogurt were the staple diet for journalists writing on the match. Was the mysterious Dr Zukhar, sitting in the fifth row, really trying to hypnotize Viktor Korchnoi? Were the Russians passing coded messages in cartons of yogurt? And why had Korchnoi hired the services of two suspected assassins? Everything, of course, was more innocent than it was made to seem. Dr Zukhar was a psychologist, specializing in detecting signs of stress. His job was to watch both Korchnoi and Karpov closely, looking for any physical signs that all might not be well with their composure. He would report back to Karpov after each game, so that the World Champion would learn how better to utilize his energy during a game and how to detect signs of weariness and lack of concentration in his opponent. The yogurt, on the other hand, was just a joke. At least, it started as a joke when Korchnoi's English seconds, Raymond Keene and Michael Stean, decided to launch a parody of the complaints which had been flying to and fro in the early stages of the match. They wrote a piece in the style of an official protest, suggesting that the colour of Karpov's yogurt might be part of a complex code, advising him what moves to play by the choice of nourishment sent to him at the board. Keene and Stean made it clear that they were joking, but as it had been in the form of a protest, the arbiter felt obliged to treat it seriously. And the 'hired assassins' were only gurus from the Ananda Marga sect, helping Korchnoi to compose himself by meditation exercises. Admittedly, other members of the Ananda Marga had been implicated in various political killings and bomb threats, and the sect was illegal in many Asian countries, but Korchnoi's friends were only there for a bit of honest yoga.

By the time the chess began, much mud had been slung and the players had built up a great deal of hostility towards each other. They maintained a semblance of decorum, however, by starting each game with a perfunctory handshake. After seven games, however, even this pretence was dropped. Mainly because of Korchnoi's attacks on the good Dr Zukhar and on other members of the Soviet delegation, Karpov decided that relationships had deteriorated below the handshake level. As far as is known, they have not touched one another since.

Those first seven games had all been drawn, though not for want of excitement. Korchnoi had even missed an easy four-move mate in game five, and Karpov had spoiled an overwhelming position in game seven. In the eighth game, Korchnoi played a risky move in the opening and was thoroughly punished to give the Champion the first win.

White: Karpov   Black: Korchnoi
Ruy Lopez

1 P–K4 P–K4 2 N–KB3 N–QB3 3 B–N5 P–QR3 4 B–R4 N–B3 5 0–0 N×P 6 P–Q4 P–QN4 7 B–N3 P–Q4 8 P×P B–K3 9 QN–Q2 N–B4 10 P–B3 P–N3? 11 Q–K2 B–N2 12 N–Q4! (*Sacrificing the KP to expose the weakness in Black's ambitious plan*) 12 . . . N×P 13 P–KB4 N–B5 14 P–B5 P×P 15 N×BP (*The lines are open and Black's king has no safe refuge*) 15 . . . R–KN1 16 N×N QP×N 17 B–B2 N–Q6 18 B–R6! B–B1 19 QR–Q1 Q–Q4 20 B×N P×B 21 R×P Q–B3 22 B×B Q–N3+   23 K–R1 K×B   24 Q–B3 R–K1   25 N–R6 R–N2 26 R–Q7! (*An elegant way to bring about the demise of the black king. 26 . . . B×R 27 Q×P+ R×Q 28 R×R is mate*) 26 . . . R–QN1 27 N×P B×R 28 N–Q8+! resigns.

After two more draws, Korchnoi equalized in the eleventh game. One curious feature of this game was that it was the only time in the match when Korchnoi opened with anything other than 1 P–QB4. Despite his success in this game with 1 P–KN3 he did not repeat the experiment. Another draw followed, so after a dozen games the score was one all. At that rate of progress many feared that the match would go on for six months. Some local newspapers and sports organizations were beginning to feel irritated at the expense of holding such an event. They even suggested that both players should be offered large sums of money just to go away. Then Karpov won two games consecutively and interest was revived. More accurately one might say that Korchnoi lost one game and Karpov won one, because the thirteenth game was thrown away by Korchnoi from a vastly advantageous position. The fourteenth game was a fine strategic triumph for Karpov:

White: Karpov   Black: Korchnoi
Ruy Lopez

1 P–K4 P–K4 2 N–KB3 N–QB3 3 B–N5 P–QR3 4 B–R4 N–B3 5 0–0 N×P 6 P–Q4 P–QN4 7 B–N3 P–Q4 8 P×P B–K3 9 P–B3 B–QB4 10 QN–Q2 0–0 11 B–B2 B–B4 12 N–N3 B–KN5 13 P–KR3 B–R4 14 P–N4 B–KN3 15 B×N P×B 16 N×B P×N 17 B–B4 Q×Q 18 QR×Q N–Q1 19 R–Q7 N–K3 20 N×N P×N (*Part of Karpov's

*achievement in this game was to realize just how many problems Black
has in this deceptively simple ending)* 21 B–K3 QR–B1 22 KR–Q1 B–
K5 23 B–B5 KR–K1 24 R(Q7)–Q4 B–Q4 25 P–N3 P–QR4 26 K–
R2 R–R1 27 K–N3 R–R3 28 P–KR4 R–B3

29 R×B! (*A fine exchange sacrifice to break through the defences and expose Black's weaknesses*) 29 . . . P×R 30 R×P
R(B3)–K3 31 B–Q4 P–B3 32 R–
B5 R–KB1 33 P–R4! P×P
34 P×P (*Now the black pawns are
ready to drop like rotten fruit*)
34 . . . P–N3 35 R×RP R(K3)–
K1 36 R–R7! R–B2 37 R–R6 R–
B2 38 B–B5 R(B2)–B1 39 B–
Q6 R–R1 40 R×P R×RP

41 K×P P–R4 42 P×P P×P 43 P–B4 R–R7 44 R–N6 K–B2 45 P–
B5 R–R5 46 P–B6 K–K3 47 P–B7 K–Q2 48 R–N8 R–QB1 49 K–
K3 R×RP 50 P–K6+! resigns (*since 50 . . . K×B 51 R×R or
50 . . . K×P 51 B–N3! finishes the game*).

So far in the match, Karpov had scored just as well from his bad
positions as from those in which he had advantages. In game seventeen, his bad games scored another victory:

White: Korchnoi Black: Karpov
Nimzo–Indian Defence

1 P–QB4 N–KB3 2 N–QB3 P–K3 3 P–Q4 B–N5 4 P–K3 0–0 5 B–
Q3 P–B4 6 P–Q5 P–QN4 (*A bold but unconvincing pawn sacrifice
against White's unusual sixth move*) 7 QP×P BP×P 8 P×P P–QR3
9 N–K2 P–Q4 10 0–0 P–K4 11 P–QR3 P×P 12 B×P B×N?
13 P×B! B–R3 14 R–N1 Q–Q3 15 P–QB4! P–Q5 16 N–N3 N–B3
17 P–QR4 N–QR4 18 Q–Q3 Q–K3 19 P×P BP×P 20 P–B5 KR–B1
21 P–B4! (*Breaking up the black centre pawns and ensuring White a big
advantage*) 21 . . . R×P 22 B×B Q×B 23 Q×Q R×Q 24 B–R3 R–
Q4 25 N–B5 K–B2 26 P×P R×P 27 R–N5 N–B5 28 R–N7+ K–K3
29 N×QP+ K–Q4 30 N–B3 N×B 31 N×R K×N 32 R–K7+ K–Q5
(*Now, instead of driving the king further away with 33 R–Q1+,
Korchnoi begins to rush matters and lets his advantage slip*) 33 R×P

N–B5   34 R–B4+ N–K5   35 R–Q7+ K–K6   36 R–B3+ K–K7
37 R×P N(B5)–Q7! 38 R–QR3 R–QB3

(*Black threatens mate on B8 and White has nothing better than a draw after 39 P–N3. Instead, Korchnoi made the most horrible blunder of the match*) 39 R–R1?? N–B6+! and White had to resign since 40 K–R1 N–B7 is mate, while 40 P×N allows 40 . . . R–N3+ 41 K–R1 N–B7 mate. A disaster for Korchnoi after his fine middlegame play in this game.

So the score became 4–1 to Karpov, time surely for him to put in the extra effort required to finish off the match. In the next nine games, however, he managed only eight draws and a loss, despite securing several promising positions. Both players were looking very tired. By now, Korchnoi had recruited his guru helpers, who were sitting in lotus postures in the hall beaming peace and goodwill to all, in order to create an atmosphere in which the hypnotic stare of Dr Zukhar would not function. Faced with parapsychological paralysis, Zukhar retired to the bar for most of the remainder of the match.

Meanwhile, back on the chessboard, Karpov won the twenty-seventh game to increase his lead to 5–2. Was it curtains for Korchnoi? Certainly the end seemed in sight. Even his seconds seemed ready to concede defeat, but Viktor is made of sterner stuff. Suddenly he achieved the impossible, he beat Karpov with the black pieces in game twenty-eight. A nice consolation prize, we all thought, but 5-3 is still hopeless. But then he won game twenty-nine too. The story began to look like a repeat of 1974. Karpov looked exhausted and the challenger had come back to life. In game thirty-one Korchnoi equalized, squeezing out a fine strategic win in a long ending:

White: Korchnoi   Black: Karpov
Queen's Gambit Declined

1 P–QB4 P–K3 2 N–QB3 P–Q4 3 P–Q4 N–KB3 4 P×P P×P 5B–N5 B–K2 6 P–K3 0–0 7 B–Q3 QN–Q2 8 N–B3 R–K1 9 Q–B2 P–B3

10 0–0 N–B1 11 B×N B×B 12 P–QN4 B–N5 13 N–Q2 R–B1 14 B–B5 B×B 15 Q×B Q–Q2 16 Q×Q N×Q 17 P–QR4 B–K2 18 KR–N1 N–B3 19 P–R5 (*The start of a very deep plan involving bringing a knight to QB5 and breaking open the centre with P–K4. The ultimate intention is to exploit White's extra centre pawn and create pressure against the black QN-pawn*) 19 . . . P–QR3 20 N–R4 B–B1 21 N–B5 R–K2 22 K–B1 N–K1 23 K–K2 N–Q3 24 K–Q3 R(B1)–K1 25 R–K1 P–KN3 26 R–K2 P–B3 27 R(R1)–K1 B–R3 28 N(Q2)–N3 B–B1 29 N–Q2 B–R3 30 P–R3 K–B2 31 P–N4 B–B1 32 P–B3 R–Q1 33 N(Q2)–N3 N–N4 34 R–KB1 B–R3 35 P–B4! B–B1 36 N–Q2 N–Q3 37 R(B1)–K1 P–R3 38 R–KB1 R–N1 39 R–QR1 R(N1)–K1 40 R(R1)–K1 R–N1 41 P–K4! (*Finally this breakthrough. Karpov could now have adjourned, but strangely rushed ahead with some crucial exchanges before sealing his move*) 41 . . . P×P+ 42 N(Q2)×P N–N4 43 N–B3 R×R 44 R×R B×N 45 NP×B R–Q1 46 N×N RP×N 47 P–B5! (*Here the game was adjourned. The endgame offers White real chances of a Q-side breakthrough*) 47 . . . P×P 48 P×P R–KN1 49 K–B3!

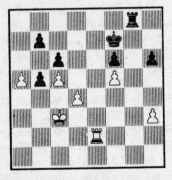

(*White's plan involves playing K–N4 and P–R6 after which the king can run in to R5 and N6. Black should defend with 49 . . . R–N8 when all is still unclear. Instead, Karpov allows White to do what he wants*) 49 . . . R–K1? 50 R–Q2 R–K5 51 K–N4 K–K1 52 P–R6! P×P 53 K–R5 K–Q2 54 K–N6 P–N5 55 P–Q5! P×P 56 R×P+ K–B1 57 R–Q3! P–QR4 58 R–KN3 P–N6 59 K–B6! K–N1 60 R×P+ K–R2 61 R–N7+ K–R3 62 R–N6+ K–R2 63 K–N5 P–R5 64 R×P R–KB5 65 R×P P–R6 66 R–QR6+ K–N1 67 R×P R×P 68 R–KN3 R–B3 69 R–N8+ K–B2 70 R–N7+ K–B1 71 R–KR7 resigns.

So it was five all and there was jubilation among Korchnoi's supporters. One of his seconds even said: 'Game thirty-two will be a draw and Viktor will win the match in the next game.' But the amazing Anatoly Karpov took a rest day and recovered his composure. In game thirty-two he produced his supreme effort of the match to win a fine game by direct attack. At the last moment he snatched the win which had looked so easy only two weeks previously. The game itself was a superb example of controlled attacking play.

White: Karpov   Black: Korchnoi
Pirc Defence

1 P–K4 P–Q3 2 P–Q4 N–KB3 3 N–QB3 P–KN3 4 N–B3 B–N2 5 B–K2 0–0 6 0–0 P–B4 7 P–Q5 N–R3 8 B–KB4 N–B2 9 P–QR4 P–N3 10 R–K1 B–N2 11 B–B4 N–R4? (*This and his next move are a clear sign that all is not well with Black's estimation of his position. 11 . . . Q–Q2 would have been better*) 12 B–KN5 N–B3 13 Q–Q3 P–QR3 14 QR–Q1 R–N1 15 P–R3 N–Q2 16 Q–K3 B–QR1 17 B–R6 P–QN4 18 B×B K×B 19 B–B1 N–B3 20 P×P P×P 21 N–K2! (*Karpov brings the knight to KN3 and plays the whole attack as though in a Ruy Lopez, despite the fact that the black KP is still on K2*) 21 . . . B–N2 22 N–N3 R–QR1 23 P–B3 R–R5 24 B–Q3 Q–R1

25 P–K5! (*The beginning of the decisive attack. 25 . . . KN× P loses to 26 N–R5+! P×N 27 Q–N5+ K–R1 28 Q–R6 P–B4 29 N–N5*) 25 . . . P×P 26 Q×KP N×P 27 B×QNP R–R2 28 N–R4 B–B1 29 B–K2 B–K3 30 P–QB4 (*The rest is easy for Karpov*) 30 . . . N–N5 31 Q×P Q–N1 32 B–B1 R–B1 33 Q–KN5 K–R1 34 R–Q2 N–B3 35 Q–R6 R–N1 36 N–B3 Q–KB1 37 Q–K3 K–N2 38 N–N5 B–Q2 39 P–N4 Q–R1 40 P–N5 N–QR4 41 P–N6. Korchnoi sealed his next move, but did not appear for the resumption. So the match ended Karpov 6 – Korchnoi 5. The World Champion had retained his crown. But that was not the end of the matter. After Korchnoi discovered that Dr Zukhar had in fact been back on his perch in the fifth row during the last game, he claimed that the game had been played under illegal conditions, contradicting an agreement reached earlier in the match whereby Korchnoi had consented to the removal of his mirror glasses in exchange for the absence of Zukhar. Law suits were heard in Amsterdam courts, but finally, after three years of litigation, the final conclusion was that Karpov did in fact win in Baguio City. A lucky decision really, or the whole of the 1980 Candidates series might have had to be replayed.

A Spectator's View
by Peter Jay

Merano – or Meran, to give the town its Austrian name – lies in the Adige valley in the heart of the South Tyrol where the rivers Passirio and Adige converge. To chessplayers, Merano evokes the complexities of the Meran Defence to the Queen's Gambit, a line introduced to tournament chess by Akiba Rubinstein here in 1924. Merano was also the place where Bogolyubov, the Soviet pretender to the world chess title in the late 1920s, chose to defect. Another who chose Merano for his home was the late Ezra Pound, a keen chess amateur whose poem 'The Game of Chess' is reproduced in the official match programme.

Two minutes' walk from the centre of the town is the Salvar Kurzentrum (cure-centre), a modern recreation and conference centre built primarily to house the thermal baths for which the resort is famous. This is where the match is being played. Entering from Piavestrasse one first encounters a row of flagpoles, with the FIDE flag flanked by those of the Soviet Union, Switzerland and Italy, representing the players and the organizers. A large billboard in the parking lot announces the match and its sponsors – the local savings banks – and close by the entrance to the two-storey building is a wagon on which stands a huge three-dimensional version of the Merano chess logo in black, red and white.

A short walk from the Kurzentrum is the Palace Hotel, a palatial hotel in the old style, with gardens in which a newly laid open-air chess set, its squares about three feet square and pieces knee-high, takes pride of place. Here reside the members of the Korchnoi camp for the duration of the match.

Korchnoi's delegation consists of the principal himself and his constant companion (I borrow this phrase from *The Times*), Petra Leeuwerik; his two official seconds, Michael Stean (England) and Yasser Seirawan (USA); three unofficial helpers, all Russian emigrés – grandmaster Leonid Shamkovich, now of the USA, and international masters Lev Gutman (Israel) and Igor Ivanov, the

Canadian champion; from Buenos Aires, Korchnoi's trainer Daniel Jacobs and his wife Inez; his Swiss lawyer, Alban Brodbeck, and his New York-based press agent, Edward Sztein, in the capacity of troubleshooters; and finally, Victoria Sheppard of the Ananda Marga sect. There was also a large Yugoslav whom I understood to be a friend of Korchnoi.

Korchnoi works every day at chess. On free days, he works from 5–10 p.m. with Stean and Seirawan, and sometimes at other periods with his less official helpers, the Russian emigrés. On match days he will spend a couple of hours at midday on chess, and before the game will exercise and meditate under Victoria Sheppard's guidance. In addition to his hotel rooms, Korchnoi also has the use of a villa at nearby Lagundo, and much of his preparatory work is done there.

Karpov's villa was at the hamlet of Scena, in the opposite direction. I was unable to discover anything about his routines; the Soviet camp was nothing if not secretive. At the Riz-Stefanie Hotel, a mere hundred yards up the hill from the Palace, and a much more discreet establishment, Karpov's delegation was staying. Viktor Baturinsky, the former military prosecutor, was its leader. Former World Champion Mikhail Tal and Lev Polugayevsky, officially present as journalists, were much more in evidence than Karpov's official seconds, Igor Zaitsev and Yuri Balashov. Alexander Roshal was the press agent, whose function was to avoid saying anything concrete, useful or interesting to any enquirer. There was also a bodyguard/chauffeur in the form of the burly and silent Pishchenko; a cook; two interpreters; and a doctor, Dr Gersanovich. This time, however, no Dr Zukhar.

I arrived at the Kurzentrum well in time for the start of the eighth game. The atmosphere of the press room was vibrant with anticipation. So it was upstairs, where the smaller of the two halls had been set up with seating for some two hundred people, and two demonstration boards on its small stage: one to record the actual game position, and a larger magnetic board for the commentator – Hort, Najdorf, Pachman and Larsen took this role at various times – to move the magnetic pieces while discussing variations. The entrance fee of 5000 lire (about £2.50) admits spectators both to the playing hall and commentary room – but by 4.50 p.m. there was hardly a seat to be found in the main hall, and the commentary room was also filling up.

Inside the hall there is comfortable seating for about four hundred spectators. The stage is cordoned off from the audience, leaving the first row of seats almost the length of a cricket pitch from the stage. The front two rows are reserved for officials, the players' assistants and their guests; Karpov's camp takes the left side of the central gangway, and Korchnoi's the right.

The stage is dominated by a vast backdrop, almost a stage set, announcing KARPOV and KORTSCHNOI with the Meran chess logo between the names. Given little less prominence on a billboard to the right of the stage are the match's main sponsors. To the left is a large demonstration board, and two manually operated clock faces showing the players' time elapsed and the number of moves made. At the back of the stage is the arbiters' table, at which sit the chief arbiter, Paul Klein of Ecuador, and his deputies, Gertrude Wagner (Austria) and Gudmundur Arnlaugsson (Iceland). In the wings, each player has a small restroom which is out of the audience's view.

All of this impressive paraphernalia dwarfs the actual centre of attention – the chess table itself. The board is screened from the audience by the two tableside pennants, miniature Soviet and Swiss flags, and by the clock; and the side of the table facing the audience is covered with a smaller version of the match sponsors' billboard. The audience's best view of players and table is found on the TV monitors, four of which are placed in the gangways on either side; on each bank of three screens you can see a close-up, sideways shot of the board and the clock, and a frontal view of each of the players.

And then there are the two enormous executive-type black leather swivel chairs. Somewhat incongruously, the players' names are writ large in white lettering on the backs of these chairs: not, one supposes, for purposes of identification of their occupants by audience or officials, but to ensure that each player has his own chair throughout the match, uncontaminated by his opponent.

Five minutes to the start of play: the hall is full. The audience looks like any mixed crowd at a holiday matinée: couples of all ages, schoolchildren, whole families, single men and women; even a nun, and an old lady in a fur coat and hat.

Shortly after the game was under way, Michael Stean came into the press room. The room was crowded and noisy, more exciting than the quietness of the hall where the atmosphere seemed one of pure meditation. The game proceeded briskly until Korchnoi's thirteenth move, which cost him twenty-nine minutes. Although his face at no stage betrayed any signs of stress, the tension showed in the bolt-upright way he often sat, and his occasional nervous fidgeting with his glasses. While he thought on, Karpov would stalk the stage or retire temporarily to his corner, returning quickly when Korchnoi's move came up.

'Viktor's got some problems,' said Stean after move 22. The Soviet corner was clearly happy with Karpov's position; Tal and Polugayevsky explored Karpov's prospects of increasing the pressure, while Baturinsky puffed merrily at his cigar. Petra Leeuwerik appeared, wearing a leopard-skin coat, and darted about nervously, looking very preoccupied. 'I'm not talking to you tonight,' she said to Robert Byrne. 'Viktor always loses when I talk to you!'

At another board, the veteran grandmasters Miguel Najdorf (Argentina) and Arnold Denker (USA) had their double-act in full flow. 'You bang, I bang! You bang a little harder, I bang twice as hard!' boomed Arnold irrepressibly. So involved was everyone in testing their own ideas that often a new move on the board would go unnoticed for a minute or two. Then, 'Ah! He's played my move. It's best,' or, 'He plays *that,* does he? I don't know . . . well maybe it's all right. Let's see . . . '

Just ten minutes left for Korchnoi's last fourteen moves. He spent five full minutes on his twenty-seventh move, and looked for a moment to be shifting in his chair most uncomfortably, but his concentration was undiminished. He moved, then stood up and glared at the board from behind his chair, hands on hips, legs slightly apart, shifting his weight from foot to foot in a kind of rhythmical trance, as if daring Karpov to make his defensive task easier by too hasty a decision. Despite his lack of time, Korchnoi meticulously recorded his moves until he had less than two minutes left. A Karpov move: Korchnoi has it recorded, raises a finger to his eyebrow, steadies his hand and then thrusts it forward, completing his move and pressing his clock button in one action.

Korchnoi stays at the board now; with two minutes left for ten moves, every second will count. A few minutes pass; Karpov is not going to be hurried: he has made the mistake of playing too quickly in Korchnoi's time-trouble before. At this critical point of the game, it is as if the position on the board between them has become suddenly alive, so fast are the moves coming; now it is impossible to keep track of them in the flurry of action, which more and more resembles a boxing match as the players' hands flick forward in sudden physical bursts. With one move to go, Korchnoi cranes his neck sideways across the board to check the precious seconds left on his clock; if he can survive the technical knock-out of a loss on time, the end of the long round will allow him to retire to his corner overnight. Karpov makes his fortieth move after a minute, and Korchnoi's reply comes in five seconds. There is a great burst of applause from the spectators: relief that Korchnoi has escaped, mingled with admiration for both players.

Karpov has nine minutes unelapsed on his clock; the playing session is not yet quite over: Karpov can either seal a move, sacrificing those minutes on his clock if he wishes to seal before 10 p.m., or play his next move on the board, which he does after a mere two minutes. He then leaves the stage and Korchnoi is alone to contemplate his sealed move, as the audience begins to make its way home.

Korchnoi spent twenty-five minutes deciding on his move, and then was advised by Klein that he must bring his scoresheet up to date before handing his sealed envelope to him for safe-keeping. This done, he retired to his villa, leaving Stean and Seirawan to work on the position. They did so until 2 a.m., and then again on the next day from noon until 4.30, half an hour before the game's resumption.

Korchnoi was rather casually dressed for the second session, appearing jacketless in a sweater as if to suggest to Karpov, you may keep me here all night but it is hardly an occasion worth dressing for. Nevertheless, he was taking no chances. Six more moves before another time control and Korchnoi has three minutes to Karpov's thirty-two. Michael Stean was watching anxiously, wishing that Korchnoi would just find the shortest route to the draw. Flushed and excited as Korchnoi safely negotiated the time-control, he said, 'It was so *easy* to make a draw, but Viktor's knight f8 was a really horrible move. He nearly gave me a heart attack! Still, it's all right now.'

When the players abandoned the game as a draw after nearly four hours of further play, in the final position which, it must be admitted, looked very pretty with the four knights prancing together, there was a general relief that such a long and hard game had ended with a result that kept the match alive. No one could fail to be impressed with both players' efforts; if the game seems less exciting to play through in the cold light of print, I must emphasize what a tremendously tense and exciting battle it had been to follow.

Korchnoi dined in the Palace Hotel's Grill Room that night. He looked tired but happy as he emerged, but could not offer Robert Byrne any real explanation for his thirty-five minutes' meditation over an easy drawing line. He laughed and shrugged his shoulders sheepishly and said only that it had not been so clear to him.

The Road to Merano

Korchnoi's quest for the 1981 World Championship had to begin with another gruelling series of Candidates matches. By a remarkable coincidence, his first two opponents were exactly the same as in the previous cycle, Petrosian and Polugayevsky. The former succumbed once more in another encounter dominated by tension and nerves, but Polugayevsky put up a far better fight. The match was scheduled for twelve games, after which scores were level. Polugayevsky had equalized with a fine victory in the very last game. An extra two games were played and Korchnoi squeezed into the final with a win in game fourteen. The amusing feature of this game was that the victory was largely due to an opening variation which Korchnoi's seconds had spotted in the morning papers. While their match was being played in Buenos Aires, Portisch and Hübner were contesting the other semi-final in Italy. For this final game with Polugayevsky, Korchnoi adopted the same line played by Portisch the day before. The Russians simply did not read Spanish, so had not read their morning *Clarin* newspaper. You really have to be up to date with chess theory these days.

In the final, Korchnoi met Robert Hübner, the highly talented West German grandmaster. This was Korchnoi's first match with a non-Soviet player for more than six years. For once he could be friendly to his opponent. Nevertheless, the strain proved too much for Hübner who withdrew from the match when they had completed only half the scheduled number of games. Korchnoi led $4\frac{1}{2}$-$3\frac{1}{2}$ and there were still two games adjourned, from which Korchnoi was hoping for another $1\frac{1}{2}$ points. Hübner had led 1-0 and later $2\frac{1}{2}$-$1\frac{1}{2}$, but a blunder in game seven and another loss in game eight finally convinced him that he was in no state to continue the match.

So Korchnoi was to challenge Anatoly Karpov yet again and the battle-lines began to be drawn up. Both quickly published books, giving their own versions of the battle of Baguio City. Korchnoi's work, entitled *Anti-Chess*, is a venomous diatribe against the Russians in general, Karpov in particular, and all others who have crossed paths with the author. He accuses them of bugging his hotel room, of planting spies within his own organization, and other similar devices more in keeping with fictional tales of high espionage.

Karpov in turn brought out his book, *In Far-Off Baguio*, to show that he too has a good line in invective. His main objects of attack are Korchnoi himself and anyone who has ever shown any friendship towards the man. In particular the gurus from the Ananda Marga who helped Korchnoi with meditation exercises are rarely allowed to survive a mention without the appellation 'terrorist-fanatics' added to their names.

So it was clear that the contestants in the 1981 World Chess Championship were in no mood to make up and be friends. The first matter to be decided was where the encounter would take place. Member nations of FIDE were invited to submit bids to hold the match. Three interested parties attended the ceremony at which their sealed offers of prize money were revealed. Reykjavik and Las Palmas had both offered one million Swiss francs, Merano had bid 800,000. But there is more to life than just money and already there was a feeling that the lowest bid might emerge the final winner. Both players had to make known their preferences before a final decision was reached. Korchnoi opted for Merano, which was where his match with Hübner had taken place; Karpov chose Las Palmas. The President of FIDE, Fridrik Olafsson, resolved to draw lots. Merano was fortune's choice and the match was scheduled to begin on 19 September 1981.

Almost as soon as the date was announced, there was a postponement. At the end of 1979, Korchnoi's son Igor had been arrested and sent to a labour camp for the crime of evasion of military service. His plight had been a cause of great concern to Korchnoi but all attempts to negotiate a release had failed. For the son of a branded traitor, life in the Red Army would have been impossible; evasion of conscription had been the only course of action possible. Korchnoi had decided that the match against Karpov would give him the chance to bring pressure to bear on the Soviet authorities by gaining publicity for his case.

On 12 June, following submissions by Korchnoi, Olafsson took a decision to postpone the match for a month. This is the text of his statement:

The President of the World Chess Federation FIDE today announced his decision to postpone the world championship match in Merano, Italy, between the world champion, Anatoly Karpov, and the challenger Viktor Korchnoi.

The reasons for his decision are the following:

1. The President of FIDE is personally and officially responsible for the entire match. He feels it is his duty to do everything within his power to ensure that both players enjoy as far as possible equal conditions.

2. In the past FIDE has tried on several occasions to assist the Korchnoi family in their effort to get permission to move to another country. Now that the starting date of the match is approaching, it becomes imperative to bring this matter to a satisfactory conclusion. During the visit of the President to Moscow six weeks ago, he had many talks with the Soviet officials concerning this matter in a final attempt to have it solved before the match. Up till now no information has been received. The President understands that this matter may take some time to be dealt with, and he is therefore now giving the Soviet authorities until the end of September to give an answer to this request.

The match was scheduled to start on the 19th September 1981, but will now be postponed until the 19th October 1981.

As expected, this statement brought strong reactions from Moscow. Both the Soviet Chess Federation, in an official statement, and Karpov himself, in an interview, attacked Olafsson's decision as incorrect. Olafsson had already annoyed them by not selecting Las Palmas as venue, but this postponement was going too far. The Tass statement:

> The USSR Chess Federation protests against the decision of the FIDE President Olafsson taken on June 12th 1981 to postpone the beginning of the match for the individual world championship which is a violation of the FIDE regulations for the match approved by the 1979 general assembly.
>
> As is known, under para 2.2 of the regulations, both the world champion and the challenger have confirmed their consent to play the match on the dates fixed, putting forward no reservations, any reasons for, or explanations of, non-availability, which may be advanced by the player or his federation, shall not be considered. (*The syntax beats me in this last sentence – WRH*)
>
> The FIDE President has clearly exceeded his authority. He justifies his decision to postpone the match by adducing arguments smacking of political overtones and having nothing to do with chess

competition and being at variance with article 1.2 of the FIDE statutes, which reads that FIDE is concerned exclusively with chess activities. Incidentally this is not the first time Mr. Olafsson deviates from the rules in the course of preparations for the match.

In these conditions, the USSR Chess Federation deems it necessary that an extraordinary meeting be convened of the FIDE executive council with a view to annulling the unlawful decision.

Karpov's interview with the Yugoslav agency Tanjug expressed similar sentiments, adding: 'I do not want to wash Mr Korchnoi's dirty linen in public and judge his moral, to be precise immoral character. But what has it all to do with the World Chess Championship match?'

Further negotiations were followed by a statement by Olafsson that the Soviet authorities had agreed that visas could be issued for Korchnoi's wife and son to leave the Soviet Union, but no precise date was given. At the congress of FIDE in Atlanta, Georgia, the decision was reached to revert to the original starting date for the match of 19 September. By now, however, the Italian organizers had insufficient notice to change their plans yet again. Finally a compromise was reached: the match would definitely start on 1 October.

Meanwhile, Karpov and friends had paid a visit to Merano to case the joint. They selected their villa, where the camp would make their preparations, and declared that they would bring their own cook (despite Karpov's expressed predilection for ravioli) and a biologist and chemist to analyse the air and water and check on their alleged radio-activity.

All quietened down until the players arrived in Merano prior to starting the match itself. Then the complaints began to flow. Karpov spent an hour and a half inspecting the playing hall and demanded several alterations to be made. He wanted a darker-coloured table, a change in lighting to eliminate shadows, and to be provided with a chair with its arms closer together. Finally, he insisted on the construction of a wooden barrier beneath the table to prevent Korchnoi from kicking him.

Korchnoi arrived and announced that he would be accompanied by two mediums to counteract any hypnotists who might be helping Karpov. He also demanded a bullet-proof glass shield around the chessboard, but this request was not conceded.

On the eve of the match, the Russians launched their most bitter attack yet against Viktor Korchnoi. It was timed to appear just before a press conference given by Korchnoi to draw attention to the problems of his wife and son. The Tass agency statement described Korchnoi as a defector 'who stoops to unsavoury tricks to disturb the psychological balance of his opponent'. He was a 'petty and stingy, calculating huckster . . . a bitterly covetous person of excessive ambitions and an inexhaustible thirst for petty revenge, a troublemaker who was not above any means to slander the very grandmasters from whom he once borrowed his experience.' His behaviour illustrated the depths of moral degradation of the man who was putting on the clothes of an ideological fighter.

Such personal vituperation exceeded the normal levels of Tass disapproval and amounted to no less than an attempt at total character assassination. He was even accused of cynicism towards his family, whom, it was claimed, he did not want to see again. The situation of the son in prison was not mentioned.

And so, they settled down to a series of quiet games of chess. Two men seated across a chessboard, each using the pieces to express his extreme hostility towards the opponent and all he might stand for. The German magazine *Der Spiegel* published a timely article to coincide with the beginning of the match. It was the edited transcript of a colloquium discussing the question whether all great chessplayers are mad; or are they simply no madder than those at the top of any comparably competitive or artistic profession?

The Games

Rules for the Match

TIME-LIMIT Each player shall play forty moves in the first $2\frac{1}{2}$ hours on his clock, and sixteen moves in each subsequent hour. The game will be adjourned after five hours' play in the first session.

PLAYING DAYS Games will be commenced on Mondays, Thursdays and Saturdays, with adjournment sessions on Tuesdays, Fridays and Sundays. Each session will last from 5 p.m. until 10 p.m.

THE WINNER The first to win six games, draws not counting, will win the match. There is no limit to the number of games.

RETURN MATCH In the event of the World Champion losing the match there shall be a return match within twelve to fifteen months after the finish of the present match.

PRIZES The winner receives approximately £150,000, the loser £100,000.

POSTPONEMENTS Each player has the right to claim a postponement of a game. Three such 'time-outs' are permitted during the first twenty-four games of the match. Notice of such a request must be given before noon on the day of the game in question.

Game One

The posturing and politics were over, or at least temporarily put aside, as the time came for the players to take their seats for the first game. At a confused ceremony, Korchnoi had drawn the white pieces. To avoid allegations of unfairness, it is considered necessary to have a two-stage procedure to settle the matter of colours. Karpov won the first round, giving him the right to conceal a white pawn in one hand and a black pawn in the other. Korchnoi gestured towards Karpov's left fist which opened to reveal the white pawn.

The opening of the game was the same as in their first encounter three years before. On that occasion, Korchnoi had looked unprepared for battle and a quick draw resulted. This time, he seemed even less ready to begin thinking about chess. His opening and early middle-game play was indecisive. Karpov quickly stole the initiative as Korchnoi allowed his pieces to become passive and tangled. On move twenty-four, Korchnoi made an outright blunder, allowing Karpov to break through in the centre and destroy the white position. The challenger seemed to have played the whole game without concentration. An hour before the end of the game, Viktor Baturinsky smiled, rose from his seat in the front row and adjourned to the bar. Despite his outwardly nervous demeanour, Karpov had played with impressive control and accuracy to take the lead.

The Korchnoi camp put a brave face on their public utterances, put forward several contradictory explanations of why he had played so poorly, and promised better results in future games. Petra Leeuwerik said: '. . . it may be good for him. He has been a bit too relaxed. And now he knows he has got to fight.' Victoria Sheppard (alias Didi), on the other hand, claimed that he had been doing the wrong meditation exercises and was too tense. Michael Stean blamed his lack of practice: 'He played cold. He is an emotional player and had not played a serious game for at least two months.' Between them they would sort him out.

White: Korchnoi
Black: Karpov
Queen's Gambit Declined
1 P–QB4

Play began promptly at 5 p.m. with both players already at the board when chief arbiter Paul Klein started Korchnoi's clock. The first move was no surprise. In Baguio City, Korchnoi had opened with 1 P–QB4 in fifteen of his sixteen games with white.

1 . . .   P–K3

Beginning where he left off three years before. The order of moves is important here. The first fourteen times in Baguio Karpov had played 1 . . . N–KB3, but changed to 1 . . . P–K3 for his last game with the black pieces. The reason for this is interesting. Against 1 P–Q4, Karpov likes to play the Nimzo–Indian Defence, 1 . . . N–KB3 2 P–QB4 P–K3 3 N–QB3 B–N5. For that reason, Korchnoi has generally preferred to delay the advance of the white Q-pawn. His early games as White in the previous match all began 1 P–QB4 N–KB3 2 N–QB3 P–K3 3 N–B3, when Karpov gave up his Nimzo–Indian intentions and led the game into the Queen's Gambit with 3 . . . P–Q4. In the twenty-ninth game, however, Korchnoi had played 3 P–K4 instead of 3 N–B3. Karpov lost that game, so changed to the no-nonsense approach of 1 . . . P–K3 and 2 . . . P–Q4. When Black has not played N–KB3, White's P–K4 has no force; the threat of P–K5 is absent.

2 N–QB3   P–Q4
3 P–Q4   B–K2

This highly refined order of moves is designed to avoid the exchange vari-

ation 3 . . . N–KB3 4 P×P P×P 5 B–N5 which had brought Korchnoi success in game thirty-one in the Philippines. Black delays development of his knight to hinder the quick deployment of White's bishop on KN5.

4 N–B3   N–KB3

Black already does not have to fear 5 P×P P×P 6 B–N5 because after 6 . . . P–B3 7 Q–B2 P–KN3! he solves the problem of developing his QB, bringing it next move to B4. White's most accurate move order, if he can achieve it, is to play Q–B2, P–K3 and B–Q3 before bringing out the KN. By playing 3 . . . B–K2, Black induces the waiting move N–KB3 after which White's Exchange Variation plan is no longer so effective. In game thirteen we see how White can play an Exchange Variation of a different type against this move order too.

5 B–N5   P–KR3
6 B–R4   0–0
7 P–K3   P–QN3

This system of development was originated by Tartakower, improved by Makagonov and perfected by Bondarevsky. Korchnoi calls it the TMB for short. The idea of P–QN3 is two-fold. More obviously, the plan is to develop the bishop to QN2, but equally the pawn provides support for a later P–QB4 advance. Since White's pawns at Q4 and QB4 in the Queen's Gambit give him more room in the centre, Black's natural plan to equalize is to play P–QB4 himself. 7 . . . P–B4 would lose a pawn after 8 QP×P B×P 9 P×P P×P 10 B×N Q×B 11 Q×P, so Black prepares to support the QP with B–N2, while also retaining the possibility of recapturing on QB4 with the QNP.

8 R–B1

Other ideas for White include 8 B×N B×B 9 P×P P×P and 8 P×P N×P 9 B×B Q×B 10 N×N P×N. Both these continuations are designed to leave a black pawn on Q4, blocking the diagonal of the bishop if it comes to QN2. In such positions Black often avails himself of the option of developing the bishop on K3 instead.

8 . . .   **B–N2**

9 B–K2

The same position had been reached in the first game in Baguio, when Korchnoi continued 9 B–Q3 P×P 10 B×P QN–Q2 11 0–0 P–B4 12 P×P N×P with a quick draw.

9 . . .   **QN–Q2**

He could, of course, have played 9 . . . P×P 10 B×P QN–Q2 11 0–0 P–B4 as before, but perhaps this time Korchnoi would have kept a little tension by playing 12 Q–K2.

10 P×P   **P×P**

Attempting to keep the diagonal open with 10 . . . N×P leads to loss of of the QBP after 11 N×N and 12 B×B

11 0–0   **P–B4**

12 P×P

A surprising decision for two reasons: White commits the crime of abandoning the centre before he has real possibilities of pressure against the hanging pawns; but also Karpov had only a few months previously shown himself to be uncomfortable against the moves 12 Q–B2 and 13 KR–Q1. The game Hort–Karpov, Amsterdam 1981, had resulted in a drastic defeat for the World Champion as follows:

12 Q–B2 P–R3   13 KR–Q1 P–B5
14 P–R4 B–B3   15 N–K5 Q–B2
16 N×B Q×N   17 B–B3 B–N5
18 N×P! N×N   19 Q–B5 Q×P
20 B×N QR–B1   21 P–QN3 P×P
22 R×R R×R   23 Q×P+ K–R1
24 B×P Q–N4   25 B–K6 R–B1
26 B×N resigns. Of course it would be extremely naive to believe that the World Champion could lose the same game twice, but all the same Hort's plan looks more hopeful than the one adopted by Korchnoi in the present game.

12 . . .   **P×P**

13 Q–B2   **R–B1**

14 KR–Q1   **Q–N3**

The hanging pawns on Black's Q4 and QB4 are a recurrent theme in such Queen's Gambit positions. Their strength lies in the control they give over the centre and the dynamic possibilities in their threats to advance. Their weakness is that they can be vulnerable to attack by the white pieces. Here the pawns are well protected and Black has activity for all his pieces. There is an immediate threat to play 15 . . . P–Q5 16 P×P B×N 17 B×B P×P winning the pinned knight. Korchnoi hurries to get his queen off the file of the black rook, but already his position is becoming passive.

15 Q–N1	KR–Q1
16 R–B2	Q–K3!
17 B–N3	

A sad admission that things have gone wrong, but the planned 17 R(B2)–Q2 would have lost to 17 . . . N–K5!, winning material after either 18 B×B N×R or 18 N×N P×N 19 B×B P×N 20 B×R P×B.

17 . . .	N–R4!
18 R(B2)–Q2	N×B
19 RP×N	N–B3

Karpov's play has a deceptively simple logic about it. He has not only obtained an attractive pair of bishops, but has also created enough room for his pieces to operate without cramp.

20 Q–B2

Trying again to bring the queen to an active post on QR4 or QN3.

20 . . .   P–N3

This and the following two Black moves are a typically Karpovian sign of contentment with his position. He has a safe advantage, so plays a few strengthening moves rather than rush matters.

21 Q–R4	P–R3
22 B–Q3	K–N2
23 B–N1	Q–N3

What Korchnoi has been doing over the last few moves is executing an elaborate plan to bring his bishop to R2 to attack the QP. He now plays the last move of the cumbrous manoeuvre, but it is already the decisive blunder.

See diagram in next column

24 P–R3??

Overlooking the force of Black's reply. And that is hardly forgivable, since . . . P–Q5 is the move White must always watch out for in such positions. Anything would have been better than 24 P–R3. Perhaps 24 N–K2 to add to the defences of Q4, or better still 23 N–K2 without retreating the bishop.

24 . . .   P–Q5!

The winning move. The point is that 25 P×P would lose a piece after 25 . . . B–B3! White's queen has no safe square off the fatal QB-file and either 26 Q–B4 B×N 27 P×B P×P or 26 Q–B2 B×N 27 P×B P×P 28 N–R4 Q–N4 loses the knight.

25 N–K2

The only remaining possibility; but now White's pawns are shattered beyond repair.

| 25 . . . | P×P |
| 26 P×P | P–B5 |

Energetically pursuing his advantage. This move not only discovers an attack on the KP, but cuts the White queen from the K-side.

27 N(K2)–Q4

27 N(B3)–Q4 N–N5 is equally unpleasant for White.

27 . . .   Q–B2
28 N–R4

Indirectly defending the KNP by creating the possibility of N–B5+.

28 . . .   Q–K4
29 K–R1   K–N1

Removing for ever the threat of a fork with N–B5+ and now seriously threatening to take either pawn with the queen. 29 . . . N–R4 would also have been very strong, but Karpov's route, too, is a clear path to victory.

30 N(Q4)–B3   Q×KNP
31 R×R+   B×R
32 Q–N4   B–K5
33 B×B   N×B

White's position, now a total shambles, could have been resigned here. Quite apart from the extra pawn, the black queen and knight combine in creating further damaging threats to the white king.

34 R–Q4

The only defence to the threats of 34 . . . N–B7+ and 34 . . . B×N.

34 . . .   N–B7+
35 K–N1   N–Q6
36 Q–N7   R–N1
37 Q–Q7   B–B2

Now all the black pieces combine in attack. The immediate threat is 38 . . . Q–B7+ 39 K–R1 Q–B8+ 40 N–N1 N–B7 mate.

38 K–R1   R×P
39 R×N

Otherwise 39 . . . R–N8+ kills him, but this, of course, only postpones the end.

39 . . .   P×R
40 Q×P   Q–Q3
41 Q–K4   Q–Q8+
42 N–N1   Q–Q3
43 N(R4)–B3 R–N4

White resigned.

The exchange and a pawn behind, there is no excuse to continue.

Game Two

Whereas Karpov has tended to put his trust in one or two well-tried opening systems during each match, Korchnoi has frequently varied his repertoire, but not with encouraging results. In their 1974 match, Korchnoi looked reliable on the Black side of the French Defence, but he only began to adopt it consistently after suffering two defeats when playing the Petroff and the Sicilian. Similarly in 1978, he had generally satisfactory experiences with the Open Defence to the Ruy Lopez, but ran into trouble playing other openings at various stages of the match.

The present game was another of Korchnoi's unsuccessful experiments. He tried to surprise Karpov with the Berlin Defence to the Ruy Lopez, something he had played only once before in his entire career. But Karpov is prepared for everything. At move 17 he improved on an obscure Russian game and Korchnoi already seemed to dislike his position. For the next dozen moves, it looked as though Korchnoi was doing nothing while Karpov was systematically strengthening his position and slowly increasing his grip on the game. At move 34 came Korchnoi's second blunder of the match. He simply overlooked an easy combination which won a pawn for Karpov. Thereafter the position was hopeless, and though he struggled on for fifteen moves after the adjournment, the World Champion was not going to let him escape. So the score became 2-0 to Karpov. In 1978 the first seven games had all ended in draws, with Korchnoi pushing hard for wins in many of them. This time he appeared quite out of touch and lacking his usual lust for battle.

White: Karpov
Black: Korchnoi
Ruy Lopez

1 P–K4	P–K4
2 N–KB3	N–QB3
3 B–N5	N–B3

When Steinitz was playing the Ruy Lopez a century ago, he used to play very slowly with white, adopting such moves as P–Q3, P–QB3, QN–Q2, B–R4 and B–B2 before pushing forward with P–Q4. The move P–QR3 for

Black was considered an unnecessary luxury, only helping the white bishop to its thematic square on B2. For that reason the moves 3 . . . P–Q3 and 3 . . . N–B3 were considered best. Later it was found that more vigorous White play casted some doubt on these systems and that P–QR3 for Black, keeping the option of Q-side expansion, was more promising after all.

By choosing this old-fashioned line, Korchnoi must to some extent have been relying on the element of surprise. He had played 3 . . . N–B3 once before, in the ninth game of his match with Tal in 1968. Tal decided to avoid any prepared lines by playing 4 Q–K2, but Karpov boldly advances down the main theoretical highway.

4 0–0   **N×P**
5 P–Q4   **B–K2**

With the moves . . . P–QR3 and B–R4 interpolated, Black usually plays P–QN4 followed by P–Q4 to support his advanced knight. This line is quite different, with Black intending to take advantage of the bishop's present placing by a later attack with N–Q3. Of course, opening the K-file with 5 . . . P×P 6 R–K1 would be fraught with danger, so Black hastens to return the pawn and castle into safety.

6 Q–K2

6 R–K1 N–Q3 7 P×P N×B and now either 8 P–QR4 or P–B4 regaining the knight is a more tactical continuation. By playing Q–K2, White announces his intention of taking on K5 with the pawn and playing R–Q1 or R–K1 to keep the black position under pressure.

6 . . .   **N–Q3**

7 B×N   **NP×B**

7 . . . QP×B 8 P×P N–B4 is also sometimes seen, though White's extra space and better pawn structure gives him the better game.

8 P×P   **N–N2**

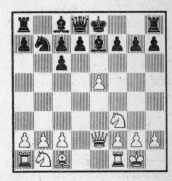

Black's opening play needs a little explanation. After all, he has played four moves with his knight, only to leave it on a very odd-looking square. In compensation for the time lost, however, he has secured the bishop pair and a potentially mobile mass of pawns. If he can play P–Q4 without immediate disadvantage, his position must be satisfactory.

9 N–B3   **0–0**
10 R–K1!

10 R–Q1 P–Q4 11 N–Q4 Q–Q2 12 R–Q3 P–QB4 13 N–B3 P–QB3 (Tal–Pachman, Moscow 1967) shows Black's plan working well. The move 10 R–K1 prepares to meet 10 . . . P–Q4 with 11 P×P e.p. when Black would have to accept the weak pawns by playing 11 . . . B×P since 11 . . . P×P would lose the bishop.

10 . . .   **N–B4**
11 B–K3   **N–K3**

Finally the tired horse reaches his destination, after making six of the first eleven black moves. This might look like a sophisticated modern idea, but it was already seen in the Tarrasch–Lasker match of 1908! In those games White twice played 11 N–Q4 instead of Karpov's 11 B–K3.

12 QR–Q1   P–Q4

At last the thematic advance, but Black's problems are not over: he still has an awkward lag in development to overcome.

13 P×P e.p.   P×P
14 N–Q4   B–Q2

14 . . . N×N 15 B×N R–K1 16 B–B5! leaves White with the advantage. Black's constant worry is that he will be forced sooner or later to play P–Q4, exchange black-squared bishops and be left with a bad bishop against a dominating knight on White's Q4 or QB5.

15 N–B5   P–Q4
16 N×B+   Q×N

The opening is over and White has secured a lasting advantage. Black's difficulties stem from two causes: his Q-side pawns are split and his bishop is restricted in scope. The real trouble is that both these problems are likely to be permanent, especially with White holding good control over his squares Q4 and QB5. So far we have

been following the game Shamkovich–Lein, Tiflis 1969–70. In that game, White had played for straightforward Q-side bind with 17 N–R4 aiming at QB5. Aided by several Black errors, he won quickly. Karpov plays the whole thing with much greater subtlety.

17 Q–Q2!

This frees the K2 square for the knight, which is ultimately heading for Q3 via QB1. From Q3 the knight keeps an eye on QB5, while also retaining influence over the K-side and centre. Karpov rightly judges that there is no need to rush the position, since Black can hardly do anything to improve his game.

17 . . .   Q–R5

The other way to activate the queen, 17 . . . Q–N5, would allow 18 N×P! Q×Q 19 N–K7+.

18 N–K2   KR–K1

The start of some planless play. 18 . . . KR–Q1 followed by B–K1 would be a better way to develop.

19 P–QN3!

Now the threat of P–QB4 forces Black to defend his bishop.

19 . . .   R–K2
20 N–N3

Not strictly necessary to White's plan, but forcing Black back to meet the threat of N–B5.

20 . . .   Q–B3

Black could hardly consider weakening further black squares with 20 . . . P–N3, even though this sets the trap of 21 B–N5? N×B 22 R×R N–B6+! 23 P×N Q×R.

21 P–KB3

This is to provide a retreat for the bishop in case of a later P–Q5 by Black.

68

21 . . .	B–K1
22 N–K2	P–KR3
23 B–B2	Q–N3
24 N–B1	P–Q5?

Black has made the necessary tactical preparations for this move, but it is too optimistic. Now 25 B×P? R–Q1 26 Q–B2 KR–Q2 would be embarrassing for White, but he can simply leave the pawn there and increase his grip. If Black could be sure of enforcing the advance P–QB4, he would have an equal game, but Karpov keeps the pawn nailed down firmly on B3.

25 N–Q3	Q–B3

The rook needs protection since 25 . . . P–QB4? 26 N×P simply wins a pawn.

26 B–N3!

Now introducing the possibility of B–Q6 to prevent the advance of the QBP.

26 . . .	R–Q2
27 R–K5	Q–Q1

The end of an inauspicious journey by the wandering queen. It would have been happier to stay close to home all the time.

28 QR–K1	R–Q4
29 R×R	Q×R
30 R–K5	Q–Q2
31 Q–K1	R–B1
32 P–N4!	

Finally ruling out any chance of P–QB4 for Black. White's control is now complete and we see the real drawback of Black's P–Q5: it has opened the route for White's rook to cross to the QR-file to molest the QR-pawn.

32 . . .	Q–Q1
33 R–QR5	Q–Q2
34 P–KR3	

Korchnoi had six minutes remaining for his last seven moves before adjournment: not great time pressure by his standards, but now he blunders.

34 . . .	P–B3?

Without this move, Black's weak pawns and dark-square weaknesses are highly unpleasant and his position may even be lost, but this move just blunders a pawn away.

35 R×P!

Such an easy move, it hardly deserves the exclamation mark. 35 . . . Q×R loses to 36 Q×N+ followed by 37 Q×R.

35 . . .	Q–Q4
36 R–R5	Q–Q2

Now we have exactly the same position as two moves previously, with the important difference that a black pawn has disappeared. Karpov now repeats moves to help reach the adjournment.

37 R–R7	Q–Q4
38 R–R5	Q–Q2
39 Q–K4	B–B2
40 Q–B5	R–K1
41 K–R2	Q–N2

Here the game was adjourned. Karpov's extra QRP was clearly going to decide matters. On resumption he prepared its victorious advance with typical precision.

42 P–R3	R–Q1
43 P–KR4	P–R4

Otherwise Black will be cramped still further by P–R5.

44 N–B2	Q–Q2
45 R–R6	Q–K1
46 Q–R5	

Curiously, White's play is much the same as the way in which he would have increased the pressure had Black not blundered away his QR-pawn.

46 . . .	B–N3
47 N–Q3	K–R2
48 Q–N6	R–B1
49 P–R4	

With Black's pieces tied to defence of the QBP, now is the time to advance White's principal asset.

49 . . .	B–B4

Korchnoi is desperate for counterplay with P–QB4, but first the knight needs protection.

50 P–R5	P–B4
51 P×P	

Better than 51 N×P N×N 52 P× N B×P when Black can hope for counterchances from his passed pawn.

51 . . .	B×N
52 P×B	N×P
53 R–R7	Q–N3

A necessary defence against the threat of 54 Q×P.

54 R–QB7	R×R
55 B×R	N×P
56 Q×QP	

Karpov allows his opponent absolutely no glimmer of hope. 56 P–R6 N–K8 might give Black a few last kicks.

56 . . .	N–K4

Now 56 . . . N–K8 57 Q–K4 is no fun at all.

57 B×N	resigns.

57 . . . P×B 58 Q–K4 and all is over.

Game Three

At last Korchnoi stopped the rot. In this game he managed finally to settle down a little and played five hours of correct chess. And that is really all that can be said. The position never looked like veering away from equality and the crowd had little to excite them.

White: Korchnoi
Black: Karpov
Queen's Gambit Declined

1 P–QB4	P–K3
2 N–QB3	P–Q4
3 P–Q4	B–K2
4 N–B3	N–KB3
5 B–N5	P–KR3 .
6 B–R4	0–0
7 P–K3	P–QN3
8 R–B1	B–N2
9 B–K2	P×P

Before Korchnoi can demonstrate his improvement on game one, Karpov reverts to the move he preferred in Baguio City.

10 B×P	QN–Q2
11 0–0	P–B4
12 Q–K2	

When Korchnoi played 12 P×P three years ago, several commentators suggested 12 Q–K2 as an improvement. As Karpov shows, this move also gives no advantage.

12 . . .	P–R3

Both preventing a later B–R6 by White and threatening to expand with P–QN4.

13 P–R4	N–K5!

14 N×N	B×N
15 B–KN3	

Playing to win a pawn with 15 B×B Q×B 16 B×P would be too dangerous after 16 . . . B×N 16 P×B P×P when counterplay against White's split pawns and weakened king ensure Black more than adequate compensation.

15 . . .	Q–B1
16 P×P	P×P!

After either 16 . . . N×P or 16 . . . B×P White could play 17 P–N4 with advantage. Now Black's isolated pawns are no more of a liability than White's backward QN-pawn. If White's QR-pawn still stood on R2,

71

he would have some advantage, but now Black's free access to QN5 gives him an easy game.

17 N–Q2	B–QB3
18 P–N3	R–Q1
19 B–Q3	Q–N2
20 P–B3	N–B3
21 KR–Q1	N–Q4
22 P–K4	N–N5
23 B–N1	B–K1

White was threatening to develop pressure with B–KB2, or P–K5 and N–K4. By retreating his bishop, Karpov prepares to bring his knight to Q5 via QB3. He also gives himself the possibility of defending the QBP by R–QB1.

24 P–K5	N–B3
25 B–KB2	

25 Q–K4 P–N3 holds no dangers for Black. After 26 B–KB2 R–Q4, White has all the problems.

25 ...	N–Q5

Not now 25 ... R–Q4 26 B–K4 R×P 27 P–B4 and White wins the exchange.

26 B×N	R×B
27 B–K4	B–QB3
28 B×B	Q×B
29 N–B4	QR–Q1
30 R×R	P×R!

The correct way to recapture. After 30 ... R×R 31 R–Q1 the resulting exchange of rooks would favour White since queen and knight work better together than queen and bishop. Keeping rooks on the board leaves the black bishop as effective as the white knight.

31 Q–Q3	B–N5
32 P–N3	R–N1
33 K–N2	B–B6
34 R–QN1	Q–Q4
35 P–R4	P–KR4
36 K–B2	B–N5
37 K–N2	B–K2
38 R–Q1	Q–Q2
39 R–QN1	

39 Q×P Q×Q 40 R×Q R×P could only be worse for White. The black bishop becomes active and White's pawns more vulnerable than Black's.

39 ...	Q–Q4
40 R–N2	B–N5
41 R–N1	

Agreed drawn.

Karpov had in fact offered a draw earlier, but this only led to a protest. Korchnoi did not wish that any words should pass between the players. Draws must be offered through the arbiters. Later in the match, both players were issued with cards to indicate when they were offering draws. The cards were inscribed in three languages, none of them Russian. But none of the arbiters could speak Russian anyway.

Game Four

Korchnoi is not the sort of man to dig in slowly after a bad start. He might be willing to play a steady draw in one game, when he knows he is playing badly, but to take more time to play himself in seems temperamentally impossible for him. Given added fire by the little row over the draw offer in game three, Korchnoi let his determination overcome his objectivity. He reached comfortable equality from the opening but then embarked upon a totally unjustified winning attempt which was easily repulsed and left his own position totally wrecked. Once again Karpov's calm rationality had earned him a point without any risks. Korchnoi was taking more than enough risks for both of them. So after four games, Karpov led 3-0 and was already halfway to victory. There was talk of this being the shortest World Championship match ever. The Soviet delegation even made a joke. They had mistakenly been issued with Italian visas valid for only one month. 'Perhaps we shall not have to extend them after all,' said Karpov. But he had twice before seen three-game leads against Korchnoi evaporate.

White: Karpov
Black: Korchnoi
Petroff's Defence

1 P–K4	P–K4
2 N–KB3	N–KB3

The first Petroff between these two players since the sixth game of their 1974 match.

3 N×P	P–Q3

We all learnt at school that 3 . . . N×P? 4 Q–K2 N–KB3 5 N–B6+ loses the queen.

4 N–KB3	N×P
5 P–Q4	P–Q4
6 B–Q3	B–K2

The battle in this opening rages around Black's advanced knight. At first Black appears to have gained a move in development, but if the knight is forced to retreat, he will find himself two moves behind.

7 0–0	N–QB3
8 R–K1	

The undermining process is under way and White already threatens to win a pawn by capturing the knight. For many years 8 . . . B–KN5 (as indeed Korchnoi had played in 1974) was the only move played here, counterattacking against the white

Q-pawn. In the first-round Candidates match between Adorjan and Hübner, however, the West German grandmaster had some success with a little-known alternative. Korchnoi follows his example.

8 . . .   B–KB4

Now two of the Adorjan–Hübner games had continued 9 QN–Q2 N×N 10 Q×N B×B 11 Q×B 0–0 12 P–B3, which seemed to lead only to complete equality after 12 . . . Q–Q2. Also possible for White is 9 N–B3 N×N 10 P×N B×B 11 Q×B 0–0 12 P–B4, but again Black's game appears to be comfortable.

9 B–QN5

And this is the very latest word of theory, played in the game Timman–Portisch, Moscow 1981. That had continued very happily for White with 9 . . . 0–0 10 B×N P×B 11 N–K5 B–R5? 12 B–K3 Q–Q3 13 Q–R5! Q–B3 14 N–KB3! and Black was already in a mess. Korchnoi has an improvement ready.

9 . . .   B–B3!

Here Karpov's pragmatic nature asserts itself. Korchnoi has clearly prepared the opening well, and has just played an innovation with which

Karpov is not familiar. Having played 9 B–QN5, the only consistent continuation would be to capture the knight, but such lines as 10 B×N+ P×B 11 N–K5 must have been analysed by Korchnoi, so why play it when the opponent has the advantage of preparation? Instead, the World Champion changes plans and adopts an inconsistent, but completely safe plan of development.

10 QN–Q2	**0–0**
11 N–B1	**N–K2**
12 P–B3	**N–N3**
13 B–Q3	**N–Q3**
14 B×B	**N×B**

Black can be quite satisfied with the opening. He has achieved his aim of equality, and in such a symmetrical position both players could already be thinking in terms of exchanging major pieces on the K-file and going home for an early dinner.

15 Q–N3	**P–N3**
16 Q–N5	**P–QR3**
17 Q–Q3	**Q–Q2**
18 N–N3	**N×N**
19 RP×N	**P–QR4**

Freeing the rook from its duties defending this pawn. Now Black is ready to contest the open file.

20 B–N5	**B×B**
21 N×B	**KR–K1**
22 P–N3	**P–KB3**
23 N–B3	**QR–Q1**

That such a position should result in anything but a draw in a World Championship match is hard to believe. What Korchnoi does with the rest of his moves before the time control is even more difficult to credit.

24 N–Q2	**K–B2**
25 N–B1	**P–R4?**

An unjustified attacking gesture which causes Black immediate problems. Perhaps Korchnoi was hoping for 26 Q–B3 Q–N5 27 Q×Q P×Q 28 R×R (*or 28 N–K3 R–K5*) 28 . . . R×R 29 N–K3 P–B3 30 N×NP R–K7 with good chances for Black. But Karpov finds a neater way to take advantage of his wild advance.

26 R×R!	R×R
27 Q–B3	R–KR1

27 . . . Q–N5 would now have lost the QP, while 27 . . . P–KR5 28 P–KN4 followed by N–K3 and N–B5 is also advantageous for White.

28 N–K3	N–K2
29 R–K1	P–N3
30 Q–B4	K–N2
31 P–KN4	P–KN4?

This leaves gaping holes in the defences of the black king. Even 31 . . . P×P 32 N×NP N–N1 would have been better. Perhaps Korchnoi was unwilling to commit himself to total passivity after his aggressive gesture on move 25. There is a Russian proverb that declares: he who says A must also say B. But if it was wrong to say A in the first place, perhaps it is better to keep your mouth closed.

32 Q–B3	P×P
33 N×NP	Q–Q3
34 P–N3	P–B3

By now Korchnoi had only five minutes in which to reach move 40. Now Karpov's attack begins.

35 P–B4!

The immediate threat is 36 P–B5 driving the queen off the defence of either knight or KBP.

35 . . . **P–KB4?**

In the spirit of 25 . . . P–KR4? and 31 . . . P–KN4? but just as weakening. 32 . . . P×P was essential.

36 Q–K3! **N–N3**

36 . . . P×N 37 Q×N+ Q×Q 38 R×Q+ followed by 39 R–QB7 would just leave Black with too many weak pawns.

37 P–B5! **Q–Q1**

37 . . . P×P 38 P×P leaves the long black diagonal open for a fatal queen check on Q4.

38 N–K5! **P×P**

38 . . . N×N 39 Q×N+ Q–B3 40 Q–B7+ or 39 . . . K–N3 40 P×P leave Black defenceless against an invasion of queen and rook.

39 N×P **Q–B3**

40 Q–K6

As usual Karpov takes the least energy-consuming way to win. After 40 . . . Q×Q 41 R×Q the black pawns simply line up to be eaten by White's rook and knight.

40 . . . **P×P**

41 Q×QP

The adjourned position, but one of misery for Korchnoi. Not only is his QP doomed, but his king is too exposed and all the other pawns are weak as well. Play did not continue long when the game was resumed the following day.

finish things off beginning with R–R1+.

| 44 . . . | R–K1 |
| 45 R–R1+ | N–R5+ |

45 . . . K–N2   46 N×P+ K–B3 47 Q×Q+ K×Q 48 N–Q6+ is just as horrible.

46 P×N	Q×N
47 Q×P+	K–N2
48 P×P	Q–N2+
49 P–B3	R–K7+
50 K–B1	K–N1
51 Q×QP	R–K3
52 Q–Q8+	K–N2
53 Q–Q4+	resigns.

A rook check next move finishes matters nicely.

41 . . .	P–Q6
42 Q–Q7+	Q–B2
43 N–K7!	K–R2
44 K–N2!	

An elegant way of threatening to

Game Five

After his disastrous start to the match, Korchnoi requested a postponement before the start of game five. Each player is allowed three such postponements within the first twenty-four games. In many of the early post-war matches, such a 'time-out' could only be taken on production of a doctor's certificate. Each player would therefore ensure that his camp enlisted a tame doctor to provide the necessary documentation. Changing the rules to allow postponements on demand was a sensible simplification of the ritual.

The events of game four had shown that Korchnoi still badly needed time to play himself in. He took no chances in this game, playing very safely to nurse a small advantage from the opening through to the endgame. Karpov gave up a pawn to reach a theoretically drawn rook ending. When the game was adjourned, Korchnoi had no winning prospects, but played on for twenty more moves, perhaps simply as a gesture of rudeness towards his opponent, but possibly also just to enjoy the feeling of a position which he could not possibly lose.

White: Korchnoi
Black: Karpov
Queen's Gambit Declined

1 P–QB4	P–K3
2 N–QB3	P–Q4
3 P–Q4	B–K2
4 N–B3	N–KB3
5 B–N5	P–KR3
6 B–R4	0–0
7 R–B1	

Apparently just a variation in the order of moves from that of earlier games, but Korchnoi soon reveals that his plan is to develop the KB on N2 instead of on K2 as before.

7 . . .	P–QN3

For 7 . . . P×P! see game nine.

8 P×P	N×P
9 N×N	P×N
10 B×B	Q×B
11 P–KN3	

A logical way to develop the bishop for the following reason: Black must sometime free his game by playing P–QB4, after which White's P×P will leave hanging pawns on Black's Q4 and QB4. White must try to build pressure against these pawns, so the natural square for the bishop is on KN2. As we shall see, Black has an

energetic way to counter this plan.

11 ...   **B–R3!**

11 ... Q–N5+? 12 Q–Q2 Q×Q+ 13 K×Q would leave Black with a most uncomfortable endgame. His QBP would be under permanent pressure and his bishop inferior to White's. Black must play vigorously and the move chosen initiates an immediate counterattack against the white KP.

12 P–K3

After 12 B–N2 R–K1, Black's pressure against the KP is annoying; 13 P–K3 would leave White unable to castle, while 13 N–K5 is brilliantly met by 13 ... N–Q2! 14 R×P QR–B1! since 15 R×N? would lose to 15 ... Q–N5+ 16 K–B1 (*16 Q–Q2 R–B8 mate!*) 16 ... Q×QP! 17 Q×Q R–B8+ and mate next move. All this has been known since the game Uhlmann-Veresov in 1970. Korchnoi's 12 P–K3 was suggested as an improvement, offering the exchange of bishops and still hoping for pressure down the QB-file. White does not fear the disruption of 12 ... B×B 13 K×B. After K–N2 all will be well.

12 ...   **P–QB4**

This move is Black's only consistent continuation, even though it necessitates the sacrifice of a pawn.

13 P×P   **P×P**

In game seven, Karpov played 13 ... B–N2, keeping the QP protected and threatening P–Q5.

14 B×B

The interesting question is whether White can get away with 14 Q×P. After 14 ... B–N2 15 Q–Q1 Black can play to regain his pawn with 15 ... Q–B3 16 B–N2 Q×P or go straight for attack with either 15 ... Q–B3 16 B–N2 R–Q1 17 Q–K2 B–R3 or 15 ... R–Q1 immediately. White's position looks very untrustworthy in all these lines.

14 ...   **N×B**

15 Q×P   **N–N5**

16 Q–B4

The alternative is 16 Q–B5 P–N3 17 Q–N1, but this is very passive and allows Black a strong attack with 17 ... Q–N2 18 P–K4 Q–R3, fixing the white king in the centre. Of course, 16 Q×P? was impossible, because of the knight fork on Q6.

16 ...   **Q–B3**

16 ... Q–N2   17 P–K4 KR–K1 18 0–0 R×P 19 Q×P N–Q6 20 Q–B7 would leave White with the advantage, so Karpov hastens to regain his pawn by other means.

17 N–R4   **Q×P**

18 0–0   **Q×RP**

19 Q×Q   **N×Q**

20 R×P   **KR–B1**

21 R–QR5

White has what advantage there is here, owing to the backwardness of the black QRP, but even if he wins this pawn, most endgames will be drawn with all the pawns on the same side of the board.

21 . . .	N–B8
22 N–B5	R–B2
23 N–Q4	R–N1
24 R–R1	

24 R–Q1 R–N8 25 K–B1 N–N6
gives White no advantage.

24 . . .	N–Q6
25 KR–Q1	N–K4
26 R–R2	P–N3
27 KR–R1	R(N1)–N2
28 P–R3	P–KR4!

Ensuring that any further advance of
white pawns on the K-side only leads
to exchanges. The only way Black can
lose such a position is to leave his
rooks passively defending the QRP,
while allowing White to squeeze forward on the other wing with P–KN4,
P–B4 and P–B5, eventually using the
advanced pawns to create a mating
net around the black king. Every
pawn exchange makes it harder for
White to accomplish anything on the
K-side.

29 K–N2	K–N2
30 R–R5	N–B3!

The simplest route to a draw; Black
surrenders his QR-pawn in order to
exchange knights and one pair of
rooks.

31 N×N	R×N
32 R×QRP	R×R
33 R×R	R–B7

If the black pawn were back on KR2
and White had played P–KN4, the
endgame would give Black problems,
though should still be tenable. In that
case, White has the plan to advance
pawns to K5 and KB5, when after a
pawn exchange the presence of the
KR-pawns still on the board gives
White a further weakness to attack.
In the present ending, White's P–
KN4 is met by P×P, with a further
exchange of pawns when a pawn
reaches B5. This always results in an
easily drawn two against one rook
endgame.

34 P–K4	R–B6
35 R–R2	K–B3
36 P–B3	R–N6
37 K–B2	R–B6
38 K–K2	R–N6
39 R–R6+	K–K2
40 R–R5	K–B3
41 R–Q5	R–R6
42 R–Q6+	K–N2
43 P–R4	R–N6
44 R–Q3	R–N4

Black must not exchange rooks, of
course. The king and pawn endgame
would be lost.

45 K–K3

Here the game was adjourned, with
Karpov sealing his next move.
Korchnoi's decision to play further,
rather than simply agreeing to a
draw, must be seen as a calculated
discourtesy, as if to say: 'You may be
the World Champion, but I'm still not
convinced that you know much about
simple endgames.'

45 . . .	R–R4
46 K–B4	R–R8
47 R–Q5	R–KN8

Molesting the pawns from behind to prevent the white king from leaving their defence.

48 R–R5	R–R8
49 R–R7	R–QN8
50 R–R4	R–KN8
51 P–K5	R–N8
52 K–K4	R–K8+
53 K–Q5	R–K6
54 R–B4	R–R6
55 P–N4	R–R4+
56 K–Q4	R–R5+
57 K–K3	R–R6+
58 K–B2	R–R7+
59 K–N3	R–R4!

Avoiding any possible problems in the pawn ending after 59 . . . R–K7 60 R–K4 R×R 61 P×R. The rook ending is far more simple.

60 R–K4
60 P×P R×P   61 P–R6+ K×P
62 R×P is also a total draw.

60 . . .	P×P
61 P×P	R–R6+
62 K–B2	R–KR6
63 P–N5	R–QR6
64 R–K3	R–R5
65 K–N3	R–QN5
66 P–K6	P×P
67 R×P	R–R5
68 R–KB6	R–N5

Agreed drawn.

At last, but now after 69 R–B4 even the king and pawn ending is a draw with 69 . . . R×R 70 K×R K–B1!

80

Game Six

Towards the end of game five, Grandmaster Leonid Shamkovich, another ex-Russian, arrived in Merano and joined the Korchnoi camp. Shamkovich has long been known for his original ideas in the openings and he seemed to have remembered to pack at least one for his trip to Italy. In Korchnoi's favourite Open Defence to the Ruy Lopez, he found a new and aggressive continuation. Karpov was on the defensive throughout the game and Korchnoi pursued the attack with a vigour that belied his wretched score in the earlier games. The World Champion held the black pieces at bay until move 39, when the tension appeared to have become too great for both players. In time-trouble Korchnoi blundered with a move which not only threw away the initiative, but could even have lost the game for him. With more than half-an-hour remaining on his clock, Karpov replied instantly by blundering back. The adjourned position was hopeless for him and was resigned without resuming play. This was only the second time that Korchnoi had defeated Karpov with the black pieces. Quite apart from the effect it had on morale in the Korchnoi camp, this game caused Karpov to give up his favourite Ruy Lopez for three weeks.

Other happenings during this sensational game included the arrival in Merano of Natalia Teysikova, fiancée of Korchnoi's son, Igor. She had been allowed to emigrate from the USSR two years ago and now lives in New York.

And we also had our first mention of yogurt since 1978. The sound of crashing glass offstage indicated that Karpov had dropped his yogurt container sometime after the opening of the game. An eventful day and, despite the double blunder at the end, a fine game worthy of a World Championship match.

White: Karpov	1 P–K4	P–K4
Black: Korchnoi	2 N–KB3	N–QB3
Ruy Lopez	3 B–N5	P–QR3

4 B–R4	N–B3
5 0–0	N×P

No more messing around with strange openings; Korchnoi reverts to his main weapon from 1978, the Open Defence to the Ruy Lopez. In this line, Black accepts certain strategic defects in his position in order to obtain active counterplay; a perfect variation for Korchnoi's style.

6 P–Q4	P–QN4
7 B–N3	P–Q4
8 P×P	B–K3
9 P–B3	B–QB4

In two of the later games in Baguio City, Korchnoi tried 9 . . . B–K2 and 9 . . . N–B4. He had renounced 9 . . . B–QB4 after a bad loss in the middle of the match, but now he comes up with a new idea.

10 QN–Q2	0–0
11 B–B2	B–B4
12 N–N3	B–KN3

The fourteenth game in 1978 had continued 12 . . . B–KN5 13 P–KR3 B–R4 14 P–N4 B–KN3 15 B×N P×B 16 N×B P×N 17 B–B4 with a difficult position for Black. 12 . . . B–KN3 is an old move which has recently received much analytic attention.

13 KN–Q4   B×N

After 13 . . . N×KP? either 14 P–B3 or 14 P–KB4 would win a piece for White.

14 P×B   P–QR4

Black must hasten to chase the white knight before White can play P–B3 and N–B5. Now 15 P–B3 P–R5 16 P×N P×N 17 B×P B×P is good for Black.

15 B–K3   P–R5!

To this point the players have been following a Karpov game of ten years ago against Savon. That had continued 15 . . . N–N5 16 B–N1 P–R5 17 N–Q2 P–R6 18 Q–B1 and resulted in a quick win for White. The move 15 . . . P–R5! was introduced by Geller in a game in the 1981 USSR Championship.

16 N–B1

The point of Black's play is that 16 N–Q2 P–R6! now causes White great problems; 17 Q–B1 would allow 17 . . . N×N 18 B×N N×QP, while 17 P–QN3 N–B6 wins material since 18 Q–B1 loses the queen to a knight fork.

16 . . .   P–R6
17 P–QN3   P–B3!

This is the new move, immediately challenging the advanced white centre rather than attempting to pursue play on the Q-side.

18 P×P

Meekly exchanging White's strong pawn ensures a comfortable game for Black. The critical test of Black's last move comes with 18 P–B3, when we see the depth of the whole concept: 18 . . . P×P! 19 P×N R×R+ 20 Q×R (or 20 K×R Q–B3+) 20 . . . P×QP 21 Q×NP N–R2 and Black has no trouble holding the

ending after 22 Q×P+ Q×Q
23 P×Q B×B 24 B×P N–N4. White
need not return the sacrificed piece in
this line, but alternatives leave Black
with a powerful mass of central pawns
in compensation. Finally there is the
question whether White can simply
play 18 P–B3 P×P 19 P×P, but here
too 19 . . . N–B6 20 Q–Q2 P–Q5
gives Black a very active game. All
told, a thoroughly difficult decision
for White. Once again Karpov takes
the safe course to avoid the sharpest
lines of preparation.

18 . . .	Q×P
19 N–K2	N–N5
20 B–N1	Q–K2
21 Q–K1	

21 P–B3 would have lost to 21 . . .
N–B6! 22 N×N Q×B+.

21 . . .	KR–K1
22 N–B4	B–B2
23 Q–B1	

White does not want to exchange his
white-squared bishop, so faces great
difficulties in developing his rook
from QR1. The black knights dominate the board, but it is still hard for
Black to create a weakness to attack
in White's position.

23 . . .	P–B4!

Reputedly the move which made

Karpov drop his yogurt. Black sac-
rifices his QB-pawn in order to create
a powerful passed pawn in the centre.

24 P×P	Q–B3!

Not only attacking the rook in the
corner, but supporting the advance of
the QP.

25 B×N	R×B
26 N–K2	P–Q5
27 N–N3	

27 N×P R×N 28 B×R Q×B would
not be good value for White. His QB-
pawn would soon fall and, with his
rook tied to the defence of the QR-
pawn, his position would be hopeless.

27 . . .	KR–K1
28 Q–Q2	N–B3

28 . . . P×B 29 Q×N P×P+ looks
good for Black, but White has instead
29 P×P! Q–R5 30 R–B4, regaining
the piece with advantage.

29 B–N5	Q–K4
30 QR–B1	P–Q6!

This advanced pawn is a constant
danger to White and provides Black
with ample compensation for his
pawn. The white queen must maintain her defence of the bishop, so cannot capture the pawn.

31 KR–Q1	B–N3
32 B–K3	R–K3
33 B–B4	Q–B3
34 R–K1	

Despite White's losing a move with
this rook, Black finds it hard to
breach the enemy position; his black-
square blockade keeps out the black
pieces. The natural result of the game
now should be a draw.

34 . . .	QR–K1
35 R×R	R×R
36 R–N1	

Black must not be allowed to penetrate with his queen to N7.

36 . . .	P–R4
37 P–R3	P–R5
38 B–N5!	Q–Q5
39 B–K3	Q–Q4?

A mistake which should let White back into the game. Instead, either 39 . . . Q–QN5 or 39 . . . Q–K4 would have maintained the initiative.

40 N–B1??
Missing the chance to play 40 N–K2!

when the threat of 41 N–B4 throws Black's whole game into confusion. When Karpov retreated the knight to the wrong square, all the Soviet seconds threw up their arms in despair.

40 . . .   B–K5
Given time to play this powerful move, the black attack now breaks through immediately.

41 B–B4
A desperate reply, but 41 P–B3 B×P! 42 P×B N–K4 destroys the defences round White's king and wins quickly: 43 N–R2 N×P+ 44 N×N Q×N 45 B–N5 R–K7.

41 . . .   B×P
This was the sealed move when the game was adjourned, but Karpov did not even wait to see it before resigning. After 42 N–K3 Q–B6 43 N×B R–K7 White must lose his queen or be mated.

Game Seven

After his loss in the previous game, Karpov changed his suit. The World Champion is very superstitious about what clothes he wears and has often been noticed to change his attire after a bad result. He appeared for game eight in an elegant dark-blue pinstripe, with red and white striped tie. At least it gave the photographers a change from the old grey suit and red tie combination.

The progress of the game nearly gave Karpov cause to return to his wardrobe. For the first time Korchnoi secured an advantage with the white pieces and really developed strong pressure against the black position. Then he launched his attack against the king too early, overlooking a hidden defensive resource, and had to concede a draw. This was one of those rare occasions on which Korchnoi was prepared to agree a draw with some play still remaining in the position. Indeed, many of the spectators could not understand why they had stopped playing at all.

With a win in game six and some more fine play in this game, Korchnoi was still 3-1 behind but seemed to be fighting his way back into the match.

White: Korchnoi
Black: Karpov
Queen's Gambit Declined

1	P–QB4	P–K3	
2	N–QB3	P–Q4	
3	P–Q4	B–K2	
4	N–B3	N–KB3	
5	B–N5	P–KR3	
6	B–R4	0–0	
7	R–B1	P–QN3	
8	P×P	N×P	
9	N×N	P×N	
10	B×B	Q×B	
11	P–KN3	B–R3	
12	P–K3	P–QB4	
13	P×P	B–N2	

At last a divergence from game five. Now Black threatens 14 . . . P–Q5! which could be taken neither by queen nor by knight. Since 14 P×P P–Q5 is too dangerous, while 14 P–B6 N×P still leaves . . . P–Q5 coming next move, White must just get his king out of the centre as quickly as possible, rather than try to cling to the extra pawn.

has the additional threat of winning the QP with N–B4.

14 B–N2	P×P
15 0–0	N–Q2
16 Q–N3!	

Such positions are quite common in this opening variation, but the black bishop is more frequently on K3 than on N2. Korchnoi attacks the bishop to gain time to bring his queen to QR3, attacking the QR-and QB-pawns, while also freeing the Q1-square for the rook.

| 16 . . . | KR–N1? |

16 . . . QR–N1 17 Q–R3 P–QR3 would have cost another move to defend the QR-pawn, but would at least have left the black rooks more active. Karpov intends to create Q-side play himself by advancing the QR-pawn, but, as Korchnoi shows, White's central play develops more quickly.

17 Q–R3	Q–K3
18 KR–Q1	P–QR4
19 N–K1	P–R5
20 N–Q3	

A comparison between this position and that of the first game is instructive. There the black centre pawns were well defended and full of dynamic potential, but here they are distinct weaklings. Quite apart from the direct threat to capture the BP, White

| 20 . . . | P–Q5 |

The same move which killed White in the first game is now a desperate attempt to hold the position together.

| 21 B×B | |

21 P–K4 is another critical line. Black cannot risk 21 . . . B×P 22 R–K1, but plays instead 21 . . . R–R4 22 N×P N×N   23 R×N R×R 24 Q×R B×P   25 B×B (*25 R–K1 P–B4 26 P–B3 Q–B3 is fine for Black*)   25 . . . Q×B   26 Q×P Q×Q 27 R×Q R×P 28 R×P when White's extra pawn should not be enough to win the endgame. Instead of allowing this simplification, Korchnoi maintains a positional advantage by simple means.

| 21 . . . | R×B |
| 22 P×P | P×P |

Now the white knight on Q3 combines defence of the QN-pawn with possibilities of attack on the K-side. The passed QP is firmly blockaded and can even be a weakness.

23 R–K1	Q–Q4
24 R–B2	N–B1
25 N–B4	

By moving the knight away from Q3, Korchnoi shows his intention to start a direct attack on Black's king. In view of what happens, he should have played 25 KR–QB1 N–K3 26 P–R4 followed by R–QB4 with strong pressure against the advanced black pawns.

| 25 . . . | Q–QR4 |
| 26 QR–K2 | Q–QN4 |

Preventing 27 R–K5 by virtue of the attack on the QN-pawn.

| 27 Q–KB3 | QR–N1 |
| 28 P–R4 | |

A necessary precaution. After 28 N–Q3 N–K3 29 R–K5, Black has the strong 29 . . . N–N4.

| 28 . . . | Q–KB4! |

A fine move, preventing N–Q3 and threatening to take the QN-pawn.

29 R–K5	Q–B3
30 Q–Q5	R×P
31 R–B5	

Agreed drawn!

An amazing position in which to stop. Black's queen cannot move anywhere safe to defend the KB-pawn and R(either)–N4 leaves White in an advantageous two rooks for a queen position. The key defence is 31 . . . R–Q1! when 32 R×Q R×Q 33 R–R6 R–Q1 34 R×P leads to a drawn ending. What both players must also have seen is the beautiful variation 31 . . . R–Q1 32 N–R5 Q–K3!! 33 R×Q R×Q 34 R×R N×R with a winning position for Black. So Korchnoi on playing 31 R–B5 indicated to the arbiter Paul Klein that he offered a draw, and Karpov immediately accepted.

Game Eight

The longest and best game of the match so far. After his defeat in game six, Karpov gave the Ruy Lopez a rest and played a Giuoco Piano, apparently for the first time in his career. An early exchange of queens seemed to indicate a peaceful outcome, but the World Champion managed to extract something from the position and Korchnoi drifted into trouble both on the board and on the clock. His last ten moves before the first time-control had to be played in less than two minutes. When he had managed to make them, Korchnoi was rewarded with a burst of spontaneous applause from the audience.

The adjourned position looked difficult for Korchnoi, but the following day, the World Champion spent another five hours trying, without avail, to squeeze a full point out of his opponent. Korchnoi refused to cooperate and emerged with a very creditable draw. Although a highly technical game, this had been a gripping contest lasting two full playing days.

White: Karpov
Black: Korchnoi
Giuoco Piano

1	P–K4	P–K4
2	N–KB3	N–QB3
3	B–B4	

There can be no greater tribute to Korchnoi's handling of the Open Defence to the Ruy Lopez than that the World Champion should give up his favourite opening.

3 . . .		B–B4
4	P–B3	N–B3
5	P–Q3	

Classical Giuoco Piano theory concentrated on the complexities of 5 P–Q4 P×P 6 P×P B–N5+ 7 N–B3 N×KP 8 0–0, eventually concluding that such vigorous play gives White no advantage against accurate defence. Recently, several younger grandmasters including John Nunn and several Soviet players have adopted quieter lines with P–Q3, interpreting the opening in the manner of a Ruy Lopez, despite the bishop's presence on QB4 rather than N5. Giuoco Piano translates as 'quiet game', and this variation has been dubbed Giuoco Pianissimo, but it can still be played with a crescendo in the middlegame.

5 ...   **P–Q3**
6 QN–Q2

An alternative plan is to expand immediately on the Q-side with 6 P–QN4 B–N3 7 P–QR4. An example is the game Nunn–Byrne, Baden 1980, which continued 7 ... P–QR3 8 0–0 0–0 9 QN–Q2 N–K2 10 B–N3 N–N3 11 N–B4 B–R2. In this variation, White gains time by attacking the bishop on N3 when he plays N–B4, and for that reason some theoreticians consider 5 ... P–QR3 to be more accurate than 5 ... P–Q3, to enable the bishop to retreat to R2 immediately.

6 ...   **P–QR3**
7 0–0   **0–0**
8 B–N3

White wishes to preserve his bishop from exchange by N–QR4. As in the Ruy Lopez, this piece finds its ultimate home on QB2.

8 ...   **B–R2**
9 P–KR3

White would like to continue with his plan of R–K1 and N–B1, but 9 R–K1 N–KN5 could be unpleasant, so this preparatory move is desirable.

9 ...   **B–K3**
10 B–B2   **P–Q4**

Black can be content with his position from the opening. In similar positions from the Ruy Lopez, White's main claim to advantage is that he can establish the ideal pawn centre of pawns on Q4 and K4, while Black's are held back at K4 and Q3. Here it is Black who is first to seize more space. Now 11 P×P N×P 12 R–K1 P–B3 13 P–Q4 would be fine for White, but Black plays 11 ... B×QP! with some advantage.

11 R–K1

Now the veiled threat to the KP induces Black to exchange.

11 ...   **P×P**
12 P×P   **N–KR4**
13 N–B1   **Q×Q**

Played after almost half an hour's cogitation. Most of that time was spent calculating the complexities of 13 ... Q–B3 14 B–N5 Q–N3 15 P–KN4!? but eventually he opted for the relative safety of a queen exchange.

14 R×Q   **QR–Q1**

White has a minuscule advantage in this endgame, thanks to two factors: first, his pawn on QB3 denies the black knight access to his Q5, while White has better chances of invading his own Q5 square with a knight; secondly, the knight on Black's KR4 is offside and will need time to get back into the game.

15 B–K3   **P–B3**

Ensuring that the KP has a permanent support.

16 B×B   **N×B**
17 N–K3   **N–B5**
18 P–KR4

A necessary preparation for kicking out the black knight with P–KN3.

18 ...   **B–B2**

19 N–K1   N–B1

Black cannot afford to grab a pawn with 19 . . . R×R 20 R×R B×P, owing to the reply 21 P–KN3! when 21 . . . N–R4 leaves the bishop trapped after 22 P–N3 and 23 R–R1, while 21 . . . N–K3 22 R–R1 B–B5 23 N×B N×N 24 B–N3 is also very good for White.

20 P–B3   N–K3

20 . . . R×R 21 R×R B×P would still have been met by 22 P–KN3 N–R4 (*22 . . . N–K3? 23 R–R1 loses the bishop*) 23 P–N3 N×P 24 K–B2! N–R4 25 R–R1 winning a piece for which the three pawns are inadequate compensation.

21 N–Q3   R–Q2
22 B–N3   N–K2

Black's meanderings over the past few moves, particularly with this knight, have been far from convincing, serving only, it seems, to tangle his pieces. After White's reply, his advantage is clear.

23 N–Q5   N–B3

23 . . . N×N 24 P×N would have left White with a clear advantage, while the natural 23 . . . KR–Q1 could have been met by 24 N×N+ R×N 25 N–B5! R×R+ 26 R×R when 26 . . . N×N 27 R–Q8+ leads to mate. Karpov's tactical control over this stage of the game is most impressive.

24 B–R4!   P–QN4
25 B–B2

Finally, a definite weakness has been induced in the black position: the Q-side pawns are now vulnerable to attack and White can open another file for his rook with P–QR4.

25 . . .   KR–Q1
26 P–R4   K–B1

27 P–KN3   R–Q3
28 P–QN4   N–K2
29 N–K3   R–B3
30 R–R3   N–B1

By now Korchnoi had only two minutes in which to reach move 40; Karpov still had a quarter of an hour, and the black Q-side is beginning to look shaky.

31 P×P   P×P
32 K–B2   N–N3
33 N–QN2   R×R
34 B×R

The rook exchange has left White threatening 35 B–K2 winning the NP, so Black's rook must renounce its attack on the BP and leave the white rook free again.

34 . . .   R–Q3
35 B–K2   B–K1

Not 35 . . . R–Q7 when 36 N–Q3 bottles up the rook and wins it with K–K1.

36 R–R5   R–Q1
37 K–K1

Now seriously threatening to take the QN-pawn, since Black no longer has a rook check on Q7.

37 . . .   P–B3
38 R–R6   R–N1
39 B–Q1   N–B1
40 N–Q3   N–B2

Not only has Korchnoi reached the adjournment, but his position even looks rather better than it did ten moves previously.

41 R–R5

The adjourned position, and one which gives Black far more cause for concern than might appear at first glance. The nature of his problems become clear within a few moves.

See diagram in next column

41 . . .   **R–R1**
42 P–KB4!

Black must capture this pawn, since his knights are unable to defend the KP. After the exchange, White is in a position to create a passed pawn with P–K5.

42 . . .   **P×P**
43 P×P   **N–N3**

43 . . . R×R 44 P×R would have left White with a useful passed pawn and a fine square for his knight on QN4 or QB5.

44 B–B3

This move indicates another of Black's weaknesses: the pawn on QB3 is vulnerable to attack from the bishop.

44 . . .   **R–Q1**
45 B–K2

Neither 45 K–Q2? N–B5+ nor 45 K–K2 N–R5 holds any attraction for White.

45 . . .   **N–R5**
46 R–R7   **R–Q2**

46 . . . N–K3 47 P–B5 wins the black knight.

47 K–Q2   **N–K3**

47 . . . P–QB4 48 B–N4 forces the black rook off either Q-file or second rank and wins at least a pawn for White.

48 R×R   **B×R**
49 B–N4   **P–N3**

A further concession by Black, but a difficult move to avoid. Now the white knight is kept out of KB5, while White's P–K5 can be met by P–KB4.

50 P–B5!   **P×P**

Any knight move could have been met by 51 P×P! B×B 52 P×P.

51 B×P   **K–N2**
52 P–K5!   **N–B1**

The only move, since 52 . . . P×P 53 N×P loses material.

53 B×B   **N×B**
54 P–K6   **N(Q2)–N3**
55 N–B4   **K–B1**

Karpov's energetic play has secured him a powerful passed pawn and, with the knight on Black's QR5 out of play, the position seems to give every chance of victory. As Korchnoi shows, however, Black still has resources.

56 K–Q3   **N–B1**
57 N–N4   **K–K2**
58 N–R6!

The immediate threat is 59 N–B5+ followed by N–R5 winning the KB-pawn, but Black must also beware of N–N8+.

58 . . .   **K–Q3!**

Now 59 N–B5+ K–K4 60 P–K7 N×KP 61 N×N K×N 62 N×P is far from clear.

59 K–Q4   **N–K2**
60 N–B7+   **K–B2**
61 N–R5

After this move, Black can escape. White's best chance to win was 61 P–R5! intending to push the pawn to R6 before playing N–R5. Perhaps Black could still have saved the position,

See diagram in next column

but his life would have been made more difficult.

61 . . .   **P–B4+!**

Far better than 61 . . . N–B4+ 62 K–Q3 N×RP 63 N×P when Black still has severe problems.

62 P×P   **N–B3+**

At last the knight on QR5 will come back into play. Not only that, but the white KP is eliminated. Defending it with 63 K–Q5? is a bad idea because 63 . . . N×P(B6) is mate!

63 K–K3   **N×P(B4)**

64 N×P   **N×P**

White can now win the RP, but always Black can liquidate pawns on the other wing with P–N5, then surrender a knight (or both if necessary) for the remaining white pawn. The game is already a clear draw.

65 P–R5   **N–B1**

Not immediately 65 . . . P–N5?

when 66 N–Q5+ wins a pawn.

66 K–K4   **K–N3**

67 N–N5   **P–R3**

68 N–B7   **N–K3**

Korchnoi was again in time trouble with less than three minutes to reach move 72. That was Karpov's main justification for playing on.

69 N–K8   **N–B4+**

70 K–K3   **N–R5**

71 K–Q2   **P–N5**

72 P×P

72 P–B4 P–N6 only brings White trouble.

72 . . .   **N×P**

73 N×P   **N–B4**

The cavalry return to save the day.

74 N–B5   **N–Q4**

75 P–R6   **N–K5+**

76 K–Q3   **N–N4**

77 K–Q4   **K–B3**

Korchnoi thought for thirty-five minutes over this move, but he can already afford the luxury. The draw is not far off.

78 N(B5)–N7   **N–K2**

79 N–B6   **N–N3**

80 N–B5

      Agreed drawn.

A picturesque final position. Black forces the draw with 80 . . . N–B2 81 P–R7 N–N4 82 N–K7+ K–N2 83 N×N N×P 84 N×N and the two knights cannot force mate.

Game Nine

Korchnoi has made a habit of finding himself three games down against Karpov before starting to fight. That was the story in 1974 and 1978, and the present match seemed to be following the same course. After losing three games with record speed, the next four had brought him three draws and a win. Yet the theory that all was now right with Korchnoi was brutally wrecked in the ninth game. A new path in the opening gave Karpov complete equality. Korchnoi could have forced exchanges and a quick draw, but instead played with the indecision which characterized his early games of the match. Once again he seemed to be trying to win a game in which he knew that the position did not justify such an attempt. Karpov seized the initiative, playing an attack of enormous power and accuracy to force Korchnoi's capitulation at the end of the session. For the whole game he had used less than two hours on his clock.

White: Korchnoi
Black: Karpov
Queen's Gambit Declined

1 P–QB4	P–K3
2 N–QB3	P–Q4
3 P–Q4	B–K2
4 N–B3	N–KB3
5 B–N5	P–KR3
6 B–R4	0–0
7 R–B1	P×P

A nice attempt to take advantage of White's omission of P–K3 in favour of R–QB1. In the position which results, the white rook is somewhat misplaced on that square.

8 P–K3	P–B4
9 B×P	P×P
10 P×P	

The position has many similarities with an old Queen's Gambit Accepted variation, considered favourable for White: 1 P–Q4 P–Q4 2 P–QB4 P×P 3 N–KB3 N–KB3

93

4 P–K3 P–B4 5 B×P P×P 6 P×P P–K3 7 N–B3 B–K2. By delaying the acceptance of the gambit pawn, Karpov has made two important gains: neither the rook on QB1 nor the bishop on KR4 is ideally developed to pursue White's aims of a K-side attack. The rook belongs on Q1 and the bishop on the QB1–KR6 diagonal for maximum effectiveness.

| 10 ... | N–B3 |
| 11 0–0 | N–KR4! |

A fine move, leading to the exchange of bishops and reducing still further White's attacking possibilities.

| 12 B×B | N×B |

Now Black's knights on K2 and KB3 will stand guard over Q4 to prevent the advance of the isolated white pawn.

13 B–N3

Played after more than half an hour's thought. Against Black's simple development plan of N–KB3, B–Q2 and B–B3, White finds an effective plan difficult to formulate.

13 ...	N–KB3
14 N–K5	B–Q2
15 Q–K2	R–B1
16 N–K4	

Were it not for Korchnoi's nineteenth move, this might be interpreted as an indication that White is already going straight for a draw. If that is not the case, 16 KR–Q1 looks the natural continuation.

16 ...	N×N
17 Q×N	B–B3
18 N×B	R×N

See diagram in next column

19 R–B3?

19 R×R N×R 20 P–Q5 would have liquidated the isolated pawn and led surely to a quick draw. In view of White's slim hopes of a successful attack after the minor piece exchanges, this was the only logical way to play. Of course, White would now be happy after 19 ... R×R 20 P×R, but Karpov refused to reunite the white QP with its family.

| 19 ... | Q–Q3 |
| 20 P–N3 | |

Again 20 R×R was correct; he does not get another chance.

| 20 ... | R–Q1 |
| 21 R–Q1 | R–N3! |

An excellent move, avoiding the rook exchange and saving the rook for Q3 to join in the attack on the QP.

22 Q–K1	Q–Q2
23 R(B3)–Q3	R–Q3
24 Q–K4	Q–B3
25 Q–B4	

25 Q×Q N×Q 26 P–Q5 N–N5 loses White his QP.

25 ...	N–Q4
26 Q–Q2	Q–N3
27 B×N?	

A decision which shows utter demoralization. After this move White abandons all hope of escape from passivity and is left only with the prospect of trying to defend his isolated pawn. 27 P–QR3 looks the best.

27 ...   **R×B**

Black already threatens to win the pawn with 28 . . . P–K4 which would still be the reply to 28 Q–K3.

28 R–N3	**Q–B3**
29 Q–B3	**Q–Q2**
30 P–B4	

Necessary to prevent Black's P–K4, but this move weakens the defences of the white king.

30 ...   **P–QN3!**

Now threatening to take the QP, since White no longer has R×NP after the exchanges on Q4.

31 R–N4	**P–QN4!**

Now the threat is P–QR4 to chase the rook away from its defence of the QP. White's reply is forced.

32 P–QR4	**P×P**
33 Q–R3	**P–QR4**
34 R×P	**Q–N4**
35 R–Q2	

This prevents the black queen from entering K7, but allows another devastating attacking move.

35 ...   **P–K4!**

With White's queen and rook away sightseeing, this breakthrough quickly gives Black a decisive attack against the king.

36 BP×P	**R×KP**
37 Q–R1	

Black threatened 37 . . . R–K8+ followed by Q–B8 mate. Of course 37 P×R R×R gives Black a quick mating attack too.

37 ...   **Q–K1!**

Renewing the threat of R–K8+.

38 P×R	**R×R**
39 R×P	**Q–B3**
40 R–R8+	**K–R2**
41 Q–N1+	**P–N3**
42 Q–KB1	

The only defence against Q–N7 mate. Now White hopes for 42 . . . Q×R? 43 Q×P+ K–R1 44 Q–B6+ with a draw since 44 . . . K–N1? would actually lose to Q×P+ followed by Q×P+ and Q×R. Needless to say, Black has something better.

42 ...	**Q–B4+**
43 K–R1	**Q–Q4+**

White resigned.

44 K–N1 R–Q8 wins the white queen. A faultless attacking display by the World Champion.

Game Ten

After the disaster in the previous game, Korchnoi claimed the second of his three allowed postponements. A spokesman for his camp described him as 'completely exhausted'. He had another fairly restful day when the match was resumed. Karpov played the Giuoco Piano again and the game never budged from equality.

White: Karpov
Black: Korchnoi
Giuoco Piano

1	P–K4	P–K4
2	N–KB3	N–QB3
3	B–B4	B–B4
4	P–B3	N–B3
5	P–Q3	P–QR3

This time Korchnoi prepares a retreat for the bishop on R2 before playing P–Q3.

6	0–0	P–Q3
7	R–K1	B–R2
8	B–N3	0–0
9	QN–Q2	

This is the position that would have arisen had Karpov played 9 R–K1 instead of 9 P–KR3 in game eight. In the meantime, he must have decided that 9 . . . N–KN5 10 R–K2 holds no dangers for White.

9 . . .		B–K3
10	N–B1	B×B
11	Q×B	Q–B1
12	N–N3	R–K1
13	P–KR3	R–N1
14	B–K3	Q–K3

15	Q×Q	P×Q
16	QR–B1	

A strange-looking square for the rook, but White wants to be ready with a rook on the QB-file if his P–Q4 is met by P×P; then the recapture with the white pawn will leave the rook standing well.

16 . . .		B×B
17	R×B	QR–Q1
18	P–Q4	R–Q2

Korchnoi prefers to accept doubled isolated K-pawns rather than open the file for Karpov's rook.

19	K–B1	K–B1
20	R–Q1	P–R3

See diagram in next column

Avoiding any possibilities of N–N5; for example, after 20 . . . KR–Q1 21 N–N5 followed by P–Q5 would have been dangerous.

21	P×P	QN×P
22	N×N	P×N
23	R×R	N×R

The liquidation has left Black with notionally weak pawns, but where is the weakness if they cannot be

96

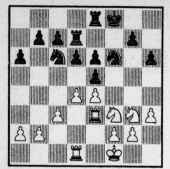

attacked? Now, while Karpov is re-routing his knight to a more promising post, Korchnoi vigorously creates Q-side counterplay.

24 K–K2   K–K2

25 N–B1	P–QN4!
26 N–Q2	P–B4
27 R–N3	R–KN1
28 P–N3	N–N1!

The knight comes to the more active QB3-square, when he will also have possibilities of playing P–N5 to secure an outpost at Q5.

29 P–QR4	N–B3
30 P×P	P×P
31 P–R4	K–B2

Defending the NP to free the rook for action on the Q-side.

32 R–B3+

Now after 32 . . . K–K2 33 R–N3 repeats moves.

Agreed drawn.

Game Eleven

Before this game began there were more disputes about whether or not the Soviets had indeed promised to free Korchnoi's family. FIDE President Olafsson confirmed that such a promise had been made, but said no specific date had been mentioned. Soviet officials in Merano, however, denied that Korchnoi had been told that his family could leave. Meanwhile, Tass in Moscow condemned as a 'monstrous lie' some Western press allegations that Korchnoi was playing to lose the championship as part of an arrangement whereby Moscow would grant exit visas to his family.

Back on the board, play regained quality with a sharp game full of theoretical interest and tactical finesse. This one was really a victory for Karpov's opening preparation; he played an improvement on some published analysis at move 23. Chess must be much easier if you have to play seventeen moves rather than forty in each session.

White: Korchnoi
Black: Karpov
Queen's Gambit Declined

1 P–QB4	P–K3
2 N–QB3	P–Q4
3 P–Q4	B–K2

Anyone hoping for a new opening from Karpov was sure to be disappointed. When he is doing well, the World Champion is even less likely to change his opening repertoire than to put on a new suit.

4 N–B3	N–KB3
5 B–B4	

For the first time in this match, Korchnoi abandons 5 B–N5, though he had played 5 B–B4 several times in Baguio City.

5 ...	0–0
6 P–K3	P–B4

This freeing move is the critical reply to White's B–B4; with the bishop on N5 it is not playable.

7 QP×P	B×P
8 Q–B2	

White plans to bring his rook to Q1 as quickly as possible to increase the pressure against the QP.

8 ...	N–B3
9 R–Q1	Q–R4
10 P–QR3	B–K2

Getting out of the way of P–QN4 and giving the knight back its support.

11 N–Q2
This breaks the pin on the other knight and threatens 12 N–N3, driv-

ing away the queen. White would be very happy after 11 . . . P×P 12 N×P with his pieces controlling all the important squares. Black must play more vigorously.

11 . . .	P–K4
12 B–N5	P–Q5
13 N–N3	Q–Q1
14 B–K2	

All this had been played by the same players in Baguio City. On that occasion, Karpov had continued 14 . . . P–KR3, but found himself under pressure in the middlegame. Since then, the position has been subjected to further analysis and more active ways found for Black. Karpov shows what is new.

| 14 . . . | P–QR4! |

Black's idea is to kick away the knight on N3 in order to secure his pawn on Q5.

| 15 P×P | P–R5! |

Now 16 P×P P×N 17 R×Q (*17 Q×P N–Q2 leaves Black a piece ahead*) 17 . . . P×Q 18 R×R+ K×R 19 P×N B×BP followed by . . . B×N+ gives Black a clear advantage, but White has a tactical trick too.

| 16 N×P! | N×P! |

16 . . . R×N 17 P–Q5 regains the piece for White with a huge advantage; after 17 . . . N–QR4 he has 18 P–Q6 B×P 19 N–B5! while other moves of the black knight from QB3 allow simply P–Q6 followed by P–QB5. Note that 16 . . . P×P? would simply have left Black with nothing to show for his pawn after 17 B×N B×B 18 N(R4)–B5.

| 17 N×N | P×N |

Now the stranded knight on R4 needs a lifejacket owing to the threat of 18 . . . Q–R4+. Even .18 N–B3 Q–R4 is good for Black thanks to the attack on the bishop.

| 18 P–QN3 | Q–R4+ |
| 19 Q–Q2 | |

The first deviation from earlier grandmaster practice. The game Portisch–Belyavsky, Moscow 1981, had continued 19 B–Q2 B–KB4! 20 Q–N2 Q–K4 21 B–N4 B×B+ 22 P×B KR–K1 23 R×P B–B7! 24 R–Q2 B×P! 25 Q×B Q–R8+ 26 Q–Q1 Q×Q+ 27 R×Q R×N 28 P–B3 R×P and Black eventually won. Korchnoi's move is a prepared improvement, but one already analysed in Belyavsky's notes to the earlier game.

19 . . .	B×P
20 Q×Q	R×Q
21 B×N	B–N5+
22 K–B1	P×B
23 R×P	

White has won his pawn, but his displaced king gives Black good chances of counterplay. Belyavsky's analysis now continued 23 . . . R–K1 24 P–N4, but Karpov has an improvement ready.

| 23 . . . | R–K4! |

As will be seen, this is a considerably

more effective way to threaten to double rooks.

24 P–N4

Black's threat was 24 . . . KR–K1 with R–K8 mate if the bishop moves from K2.

24 . . .   **P–N4!**

With the rook on QR4, this move would make no sense since the reply P×P would leave it cut off. As played, it is the most effective way to develop the bishop on QB1.

25 P×P   **B–N2**

26 P–B3

There is a tempting sacrifice of the exchange with 26 R×B B×R 27 P–B3, but Black's resources are adequate after 27 . . . KR–K1. One plausible continuation is 28 N–B3 R–K6 29 N–Q5 R×B 30 N×P+ K–B1 31 N×R R×N 32 K–B2 R–N1 33 P–N6 R–N2 34 R–KB4 R×P 35 K–N1 R×P 36 K×B with a totally drawn rook and pawn endgame.

26 . . .   **KR–K1**

27 B–Q1

The bishop must remain on the defence of the BP.

27 . . .   **R×P**

The complications have cleared to reach a position in which the active black bishop pair provides full compensation for the pawn minus.

28 K–N2	**K–N2**
29 K–B2	**B–R4**
30 R–B1	**R–K2**

Curiously, neither side can improve his position.

31 P–R3	**P–R3**
32 B–B2	**R–B2**
33 R–QB4	**R×R**
34 P×R	**R–N5**
35 P–B5	**B–B3**

     Agreed drawn.

Black can always force a draw after 36 R–QR1 with 36 . . . R–QB5 37 B–N3 R–N5 38 B–Q1 R–QB5. The threat of 39 . . . B×N followed by R×P gives White nothing better than to repeat moves. Equally, 36 R–QR1 R–QB5 37 B–N3 R–N5 38 R–R3 gives White nothing after 38 . . . R–KB5 39 B–Q1 B–N5. With the extra pawn on QB5 so blockaded and so vulnerable, White's winning chances from such a position must be nil.

Game Twelve

Anyone following the progress of this match in the hope of some titillating side-shows *à la Baguio* must have been very disappointed until today. Korchnoi had been remarkably controlled and subdued, and indeed his whole team lacked the over-exuberance which had characterized their cheerful behaviour in the Philippines. Perhaps the meditation exercises which Korchnoi was performing before each game really had calmed him down.

Not today, though. After twenty-five minutes of the game Korchnoi was seen to snarl a string of words at the World Champion. The arbiter intervened and a brief row ensued. The challenger, it seemed, was complaining about his opponent's habit of swivelling in his chair. What he had actually said was: 'Stop squirming in your damn seat, you little worm,' or the Russian equivalent thereof. (Nobody was quite sure of the precise English translation of Korchnoi's final pejorative term. Etymologists in the press-room established it to be a double diminutive of a word meaning something that crawls around in soil. Korchnoi's own suggestion was 'little creep'.)

Whatever the exact meaning, the Soviet delegation were none too pleased and submitted an official protest about the incident, demanding that Korchnoi be punished and that he apologize. Korchnoi submitted a counter-protest, demanding that Karpov cease his swivelling. The jury met for the first time in the match and in a true spirit of fair play agreed with both men. Korchnoi was warned about his behaviour and threatened with a fine of 15,000 Swiss francs (over £4000) if he did it again; Karpov was politely asked to keep still in his chair.

Later, Korchnoi's lawyer and head of delegation, Alban Brodbeck, sent a long telex message to Olafsson complaining about the threat of a fine. Olafsson declined to enter a legal argument and agreed to delete the last line of the jury's statement which referred to the proposed punishment. Since FIDE rules for the World Championship recommend the use of fixed chairs rather than swivels, rockers, shooting-sticks or hammocks, the whole affair ought never to have happened.

Back on the chessboard, Korchnoi had a narrow escape. His opening play led to a passive position and Karpov established the advantage on both wings. Rather than play a K-side attack, the World Champion settled for pressure on the other flank. Eventually this won him a pawn, but Korchnoi squirmed successfully to crawl out into a drawn endgame. All in all, quite an eventful day.

White: Karpov
Black: Korchnoi
English Opening
  1 P–QB4

So 1 P–K4 finally earns a rest. Some of the Soviet delegations were heard to ask visiting grandmasters if they knew anything against the Open Defence to the Ruy Lopez. Was Karpov really running out of openings with White? See game thirteen for the answer.

  1 . . .   **N–KB3**
  2 N–QB3   **P–Q4**

One of Korchnoi's favourite moves, in the spirit of the Grünfeld Defence. Black offers White more pawns in the centre in the belief that these can be undermined and attacked later in the game.

  3 P×P   **N×P**
  4 N–B3

In the same position in the thirtieth game of the previous match, Karpov had played 4 P–KN3 P–KN3 5 B–N2 N×N 6 NP×N. This time he has another diagonal in mind for his bishop.

  4 . . .   **N×N**

4 . . . P–KN3 is also often played here, but that gives White the opportunity for either 5 Q–R4+ followed by Q–Q4 or 5 P–K4 N×N 6 QP×N Q×Q+ 7 K×Q when the black bishop on KN2 has nothing

to do in the resulting endgame. By exchanging knights first, Korchnoi lessens White's options but also cuts down his own possibilities.

  5 NP×N   **P–KN3**
  6 P–Q4   **P–QB4**
  7 P–K3

7 P–K4 would lead to a well-known position from the Grünfeld Defence in which Black's bishop at KN2 plays a crucial role in attacking the big white centre. By keeping the pawn at K3 for the moment, Karpov ensures a solid central formation to frustrate Black's attacking intentions.

  7 . . .   **B–N2**
  8 B–N5+   **N–Q2**

I prefer 8 . . . B–Q2; Black's play against the centre is easier with the knight developed on B3.

  9 0–0   **0–0**
  10 P–QR4!

Restraining the black pawns from advancing to QR3 and QN4 while also threatening to hamper Black's Q-side development by playing P–R5. Ideally Black would like knight on QB3 and queen on B2 in such a position, with the bishop having the option of QN2 or KN5 and the knight able to play to QR4 and perhaps later to QB5.

10 . . .   P–QR3

Not a pleasant decision to take since this leaves the black Q-side pawns vulnerable to attack. 10 . . . P–N3 looks better.

11 B–Q3	P–N3
12 R–N1	B–N2
13 P–K4!	

The time is ripe for this pawn to advance. Against such a pawn centre, Black always wants his knight on QB3 and bishop on KN5. Against his present restrained scheme of development, White has no fears that his pawns will want for support.

13 . . .	Q–B2
14 R–K1	P–K3
15 P–K5	P–R3

Another sign of passivity, but 15 . . . KR–Q1 16 B–KN5 is. very unpleasant for Black.

16 P–R4!	KR–Q1
17 B–KB4	

The beginning of some inconsistent play by Karpov. Having embarked upon an energetic attacking course in the previous move, he now appears to change his mind and switch his attention to the other wing. The consistent continuation is 17 P–KR5!, threatening to weaken Black's K-side seriously with P×P. After 17 . . . P–KN4, Tal was strongly advocating the piece sacrifice 18 N×P! P×N 19 B×NP,

when the threats of B×R or P–R6 and Q–N4 make life very unpleasant for Black. As usual when three points ahead, Karpov feels no urge to take any risks.

17 . . .   N–B1
18 B–K3

Black threatened to win the QP with B×N followed by P×P, so he retracts his previous move. Now that the black knight has opted for K-side defence, White shifts his action to the other wing.

18 . . .	QR–N1
19 Q–K2	B–QB3
20 B×QRP	P×P
21 P×P	B×RP

Korchnoi does not entertain great hopes for the survival of his straggling QN–pawn, but has a clear plan to save the game based on a blockade of the Q4 square.

22 N–Q2   Q–B3

Threatening to win the bishop by playing P–QN4.

23 KR–QB1	Q–R1
24 B–Q3	B–QB3
25 P–B3	P–QN4!

The pawn offers its life to save the side. After 26 B×QNP R×B 27 R×R Q–R3! the pin on the diagonal costs White material. In any case, Karpov wants to retain his white-squared bishop.

26 N–N3   QR–B1

Confirming that he is always content to give up the QNP if that results in an exchange of white-squared bishops.

27 N–B5   N–Q2
28 N–K4   B×N

An unfortunate necessity; the knight could not be allowed to reach Q6 or KB6. Now Black has exchanged one of the defenders of the vital Q4 square, but the knight is on its way to hold up the advance of the white QP.

29 R×R   Q×R
30 B×B

30 P×B would solve the problem of controlling Q5, but the KP would then have inadequate protection for White to enforce P–Q5.

30 . . .   Q–B5
31 B–Q3   Q–B6
32 B×QNP

32 R×P would have allowed 32 . . . N×P! and the bishop on Q3 is hanging.

32 . . .   N–N3
33 Q–Q3   N–Q4

The knight reaches the vital square and Black's salvation is in sight.

34 B–B2   P–R4
35 Q×Q   N×Q
36 R–N3   N–Q8!

Eliminating the black-squared bishop to ensure that opposite-coloured bishops remain on the board to ease Black's drawing task.

37 R–Q3   N×B
38 K×N   R–N1
39 B–B4   R–N7+
40 K–N3   R–N5
41 R–B3

41 B–N3 could have been answered

by 41 . . . R×P! 42 R×R B×P+ 43 R–B4 K–N2 with an extraordinary positional draw since White can never break the pin on his rook.

41 . . .   R–N1

The sealed move. White would only have chances to win if he could enforce P–Q5 without allowing an exchange of rooks, but that is impossible and the game drifts quickly to a draw.

42 P–B4

42 B–N3 would allow Black's trick of 42 . . . R–Q1 43 R–Q3 R×P! again, while 42 R–Q3 R–N5 would simply repeat position, so White has no option but to allow the drawing pin on the QB-file.

42 . . .   R–QB1
43 K–B2   B–B1
44 K–K3   B–N5
45 R–B1

45 R–B2 B–K8 wins the white RP.

45 . . .   B–R6
46 R–B2

Once again 46 R–QR1 B–K2 lets Black equalize the material, though 46 . . . R×B 47 R×B would also be a draw.

46 . . .   B–N5

Renewing the threat of B–K8. The white king is not going to be allowed time to come to Q3, defending the bishop and relieving the rook.

47 R–B1

Agreed drawn.

47 . . . B–R6 forces White to repeat moves.

Game Thirteen

Karpov is known to be superstitious about the clothes he wears and he does not like to play on Mondays, but until this game he had no reason to fear the number thirteen. In 1978 the thirteenth game brought him his luckiest win of the match. This time he was crushed in a powerfully played game by Korchnoi. They had begun the game with the chief arbiter gently asking Karpov not to move about in his chair. The World Champion sat rigidly in his seat throughout the game. Korchnoi spent much of the time offstage, studying the position on demonstration boards and returning only to make his moves. That behaviour he had learnt from Spassky who had preferred not to share a board with Korchnoi himself in 1978.

The challenger tried a new tack in the opening, playing an Exchange Variation which had frequently occurred in the World Championship match of 1963 between Botvinnik and Petrosian. Karpov played the theoretically recommended moves, but on looking at his position at the end of them, he discovered that all was not well. Korchnoi quickly developed a strong attack but the World Champion ingeniously complicated the position. In the complexities, however, he suffered decisive material losses and resigned at the adjournment. Later analysis showed that in the middle of the messy portion of the game, Karpov had missed a drawing combination. Nonetheless a fine game by Korchnoi and a struggle well worthy of the occasion.

White: Korchnoi
Black: Karpov
Queen's Gambit Declined

1 P–QB4	P–K3
2 N–QB3	P–Q4
3 P–Q4	B–K2
4 P×P	

The main surprise about this move is that Korchnoi has never played it previously against Karpov. The merit of the pawn exchange is that it imbalances the pawn structure and leads to the type of heavy strategic battle which Korchnoi relishes. Equally, Karpov has demonstrated the impressive extent of his preparation in

the standard variations with 4 N–B3.
This line has the advantage of being
considerably less well researched. On
the minus side, Black's development,
particularly of his QB is considerably
eased by the pawn exchange.

4 ...   P×P
5 B–B4   P–QB3
6 P–K3

Korchnoi tried the ambitious plan of
6 Q–B2 P–KN3! 7 0–0–0 B–KB4 in
one of his match games against
Spassky in 1968. The result was not
encouraging: Black crashed through
with a Q-side attack.

6 ...   B–KB4

7 P–KN4!?
Meekly consenting to the exchange
of bishops after 7 B–Q3 B×B
8 Q×B N–B3 offers White little
hope of advantage. This bold pawn
move is the only way to try to take
advantage of Black's bishop development.

7 ...   B–K3
After 7 ... B–N3, Botvinnik ana-
lysed 8 P–KR4!? B×P (or 8 ... P–
KR4 9 P–N5 and the black knight on
KN1 is stuck in his stable), 9 Q–N3
P–QN3 10 R×B Q×R 11 N×P!

P×N 12 Q×QP and White is winning.

8 P–KR3
Having thrust forward the KN-pawn,
White needs to defend it in order to
develop his KN. The idea of P–KR3
and P–KN4 as a middlegame attacking plan is quite logical, but to play it
so early in the opening might be cri-
ticized as too commital.

8 ...   N–B3
9 B–Q3   P–B4

If Black develops quietly with
9 ... QN–Q2, White continues with
N–B3, Q–B2 and 0–0–0, playing for a
K-side attack. The move 9 ... P–B4
discourages White from trying to
castle Q-side. It should be the correct
move, since chess dogma demands
that a premature wing advance be
countered by action in the centre.
The question is whether White's centre is sufficiently strong to withstand
the pressure and keep the position
closed.

10 N–B3   N–B3
11 K–B1

The Q-side is no longer safe for the
white king, so he makes for security
on KN2. There is no need to castle,
since the rook is not badly placed on
KR1.

11 ...   0–0
12 K–N2   R–B1

The first divergence from the fourteenth game of the 1963 Botvinnik–Petrosian match. Petrosian had
played 12 ... P×P 13 KN×P N×N
14 P×N when White advanced
pawns gave him a troublesome
advantage in space. Karpov's move
was recommended as an improvement at the time of the earlier match.

13 QR–B1   R–K1

A rather casual move which leads to difficulties for Black. I prefer 13 . . . P–QR3, keeping the white knight out of its QN5, while giving Black the possibility of a Q-side advance with P–B5 and P–QN4.

14 P×P   **KB×P**
15 N–QN5   **B–B1**
16 KN–Q4!

Faced with this position Karpov sank into deep thought for nearly forty minutes. White's threat is simply 17 N×N and 18 N×RP, but Black's problems are deeper than mere tactics. The root of the trouble is that his pieces do not have enough room to cooperate effectively. For example the natural 16 . . . Q–Q2 allow 17 N×B P×N (*other recaptures lose to B–B5*) 18 P–N5! and the black knight has no square since 18 . . . N–K5 19 B×N wins a piece. Equally 16 . . . Q–N3 17 Q–N3 N×N 18 P×N! leaves White with the terrible threat of B–B7.

16 . . .   **N×N**
17 R×R   **Q×R**
18 P×N!

A very fine move, giving White greater advantage than the appar-

ently more natural recapture with the knight.

18 . . .   **Q–Q2**
19 N–B7   **R–B1**
20 N×B   **P×N**

20 . . . Q×N would have lost the exchange to 21 B–B5, but now White has a fine bishop pair and a weakness on Black's K3 upon which to concentrate his attention.

21 R–K1   **P–QR3**
22 P–N5   **N–K5!**

Black must avoid being driven into total passivity while White builds up his attack. Now 23 B×N P×B 24 R×P Q–Q4 gives Black fine counterplay.

23 Q–N4   **B–N5**
24 R–K2   **R–B1**

Looking for counterplay down the KB-file.

25 P–B3   **Q–KB2**
26 B–K5   **N–Q7!**

26 . . . N–Q3 27 P–R3 would have lost without a fight, while 26 . . . N×P 27 Q×N Q×P+ 28 K–R2 leaves Black no time to take the bishop owing to the mate threat on KN2.

27 P–R3   **N×P**

Still fighting for his life. 28 P×B would be met by 28 . . . N–K8+! when 29 R×N loses to 29 . . . Q–B7+ while 29 K–R2 N×B is fine for Black.

28 P–N6   **P×P**
29 B–N3

Korchnoi takes a move to defend against the threat of 29 . . . N–K8+ which would now be met by 30 R×N! B×R 31 B×B when the two white bishops are far better than Black's rook and pawns. After Karpov's reply, he is clearly lost. Yet this is where he missed his chance to save

the game.

29 . . .   **B–K2?**

The right move was 29 . . . N–R5+!! when 30 Q×N Q–B6+ 31 K–R2 Q×B or 30 B×N Q–B8+ 31 K–R2 B–Q3+ 32 B–N3 R–B7+ 33 R×R Q×R+ would both be bad for White. So he must play 30 K–R2 N–B6+ 31 K–R1 when again 31 . . . N–R5! and everything miraculously holds together: 32 B×N Q–B8+ 33 K–R2 B–Q3+ as before, or 32 R–KB2 N–B4 33 P×B N×B+, or 32 Q×N Q–B6+ 33 R–N2 Q×B 34 P×B R–B8+ 35 K–R2 Q–Q8 with at least enough counterplay for Black in every case.

30 R–KB2

The pin on the black knight wins material.

30 . . .   **N–K8+**

31 K–R1   **Q×R**

Desperation, but 31 . . . N–B6 32 B–K2 kills the knight while 31 . . . Q–K1 is met by 32 R×R+ and 33 B×N.

32 B×Q   **N×B**

33 Q×P+   **R–B2**

Black has rook, knight and pawn for the queen, but his knight is trapped inside the enemy lines. Korchnoi now cleverly uses the pin on the black rook to help him win the knight.

34 B–N3   **N×P**

35 Q×QP   **B–B3**

White threatened to win the knight with 36 Q–N3. Now that move can be met by 36 . . . B×P.

36 B–Q6

Threatening 37 Q–K6 and 38 Q–K8+ winning the rook. Black can only try to advance both his KN-pawns to create a square for the king on N2.

36 . . .   **P–KN4**

37 Q–N3!   **B×P**

38 Q–K6   **P–KN3**

39 Q–K8+   **K–N2**

40 B–K5+

Finally revealing why the black bishop was lured to Q5 on move 37.

40 . . .   **B×B**

41 Q×B+   **K–R2**

Here the game was adjourned, but **Black resigned** without resuming play. After 42 Q×N the endgame is quite hopeless. Keene suggested a very convincing line to demolish Black's only attempt to set up a blockade: 42 . . . P–R4 43 P–QR4 R–B4 44 Q×P+ K–N1 45 K–N2 K–R1 46 K–N3 K–N1 47 K–N4 K–R1 48 Q–Q7! K–N1 49 Q×R! P×Q+ 50 K×NP and the white king heads straight for the QR-pawn after taking the KB-pawn, with an easy win.

Game Fourteen

What happens when you cut a worm in half? Of course, it turns right round and bites your head off. That, at any rate, was what Karpov did to Korchnoi in this game to revenge himself for the insult of game thirteen and the injury of game fourteen. At last the World Champion was ready to reveal his preparation against the Open Defence to the Ruy Lopez. In a position he must have analysed during the match three years ago, Korchnoi seized up completely and began to think for over an hour on one move. Four moves later he was completely lost. Once again the challenger seemed to have lost the capacity to take wholly rational decisions without letting subjective considerations interfere.

White: Karpov
Black: Korchnoi
Ruy Lopez

1	P–K4		P–K4
2	N–KB3		N–QB3
3	B–N5		P–QR3
4	B–R4		N–B3
5	0–0		N×P
6	P–Q4		P–QN4
7	B–N3		P–Q4
8	P×P		B–K3
9	QN–Q2		

A new fashion for Merano, but played twice in Baguio City. White takes immediate measures to dislodge the knight from Black's K5.

9	. . .		N–B4
10	P–B3		P–Q5

10 . . . N×B 11 N×N leaves White with a pleasant hold on the black squares, especially Q4 and QB5. 10 . . . P–Q5 has long been thought to solve Black's problems by central exchanges.

11 B×B

Game ten in Baguio saw Korchnoi (and almost everyone else) startled by the move 11 N–N5!? After a long thought, he declined the offer, but later analysis showed that 11 . . . Q×N   12 Q–B3 0–0–0! 13 Q×N Q×P is not bad for Black, though the complications are enormous.

11	. . .		N×B
12	P×P		N(B3)×QP
13	N–K4		

White's last three moves have consisted of two exchanges followed by a natural centralizing move of the

position. 16 . . . Q–B1 was essential.

knight. All this must have come under detailed inspection in Baguio. So why did Korchnoi now sink into thought for seventy-eight minutes? The likely explanation is a sneaking fear that the Soviet camp had somehow discovered the details of the preparation in Baguio and were now ready with a strong reply. Those who were with Korchnoi three years ago have disagreed about what they analysed there, but the main area of investigation seems to have been the following variation: 13 . . . Q–Q4 14 N×N Q×N(K5) 15 N×N P×N 16 R–K1 Q–B4 and now one possibility is 17 P–KN4!? Q–N3 18 Q–B3 R–Q1 19 Q–B6+ K–B2 20 Q×BP+ B–K2 when Black has good play for his pawn. Rejecting that line, Korchnoi finally played a simple developing move.

13 . . .	B–K2
14 B–K3	N×N+?

The cause of Black's further problems. This just encourages White's queen to a good square. In game sixteen, Korchnoi improved with 14 . . . N–KB4!

15 Q×N	0–0
16 KR–Q1	Q–K1

Another mistake in an already bad

17 N–B6+!

Effectively sealing Black's fate before he is out of the opening.

17 . . .	B×N

Accepting the sacrifice with 17 . . . P×N 18 P×P B–Q3 leaves the black king too exposed to live: 19 R–Q5 K–R1 20 R–KR5 and Black is defenceless against White's mating plans on KR7. Vacating KB1 for the knight with 20 . . . R–KN1 allows the nice finish 21 R×P+! K×R 22 Q–R5 mate.

18 P×B	Q–B1

The queen's presence on K1 prevented the defence 18 . . . P–N3 when 19 B–R6 would have won the exchange.

19 P×P	R–Q1

Leaving the white pawn on N7 is safer than taking it and exposing the king to attack on the N-file and the black squares. Now at least the white pawn offers the black king some sort of shelter, but the whole position is already beyond hope of salvation.

20 P–KR4!

Karpov allows himself the simple luxury of advancing this pawn in support of its friend.

20 . . .	P–QB4	31 R–B1	Q–Q4
21 QR–B1	Q–B2	32 Q–N3	Q–K5
22 P–R5	Q–K4	33 Q–B2	Q×Q
23 P–R6	Q×QNP	34 R×Q	

Black has regained his pawn, but now the protected pawn on N7 gives White the chance to launch a decisive attack.

24 R–Q7!

The threat of mate on KB7 forces Black to let the white queen into his position.

24 . . .	R×R		
25 Q×R+	R–Q1		
26 Q×P	Q–K7		

Threatening 27 . . . R–Q8+ forcing a draw by perpetual check.

27 R–B1	R–Q8
28 Q–R8+	R–Q1
29 Q–B6	

Now the black rook is totally tied to the back rank for fear of Q–K8.

29 . . .	P–N5
30 Q–R4	Q–Q6

With an extra pawn and Black's king unable to join in the game, the endgame must be won for White. Karpov shows how to do it with minimum fuss.

34 . . .	P–B4
35 P–B4	

Not 35 B×P? R–QB1 and Black wins a piece.

35 . . .	K–B2
36 P–N4!	R–Q4

36 . . . P×P 37 P–B5 would leave Black crushed by the avalanche of pawns.

37 P×P	R×P
38 R–Q2!	R–B3
39 R–Q7+	K–N1
40 P–B5!	R×BP
41 R–K7	

The double threat of R×N and R–K8+ wins a piece. Resigning here would have been polite, but Korchnoi preferred an alternative approach.

41 . . .	N×P
42 R×N+	K–R1
43 R–QB7	K–N1
44 B×P	R–N4+
45 K–B2	R–N3
46 B–K3	

Adjourned here, but of course **Black resigned** the hopeless task before resumption.

Game Fifteen

With the score at 5-2 to Karpov, the match could finish at any moment. Confident predictions had been made that Korchnoi would take the last of his three postponements after the demoralizing defeat in game fourteen, but they were wrong. He turned up to play as usual. The Soviet delegation began to drop heavy hints that their man was about to triumph. From now onwards, their number began to be augmented with dignitaries to adorn the closing ceremony. Karpov's wife, Irina, and the deputy minister for sport were the first to arrive. Korchnoi, we knew, would do his best to keep them hanging around. A similar crowd had assembled when Karpov led 5-2 in Baguio; they were almost disappointed.

In today's game, Karpov defended an English Opening for the first time. Korchnoi had some advantage and even won a pawn, but Karpov's solid defence was equal to the occasion. By the adjournment, the draw was clear.

White: Korchnoi
Black: Karpov
English Opening

| 1 P–QB4 | N–KB3 |
| 2 N–QB3 | P–K4 |

'No, Mr Korchnoi, I am not ready for your Queen's Gambit again; but my boys are working on it and I'll let you know.'

| 3 N–B3 | N–B3 |
| 4 P–KN3 | B–N5 |

This bishop development has become one of the most popular lines against the English in recent years. Black's idea is just to play B×N and P–K5, with 0–0, R–K1 and P–Q3 to complete his formation. White's usual plan of pressure on the long white diagonal becomes difficult to operate. Curiously, this same position was reached twice in Baguio City, once with Korchnoi White and once with the players having changed colours.

| 5 N–Q5 | B–B4 |

Having lured White's knight, perhaps prematurely, to Q5, Black is happy to move his bishop again.

6 B–N2	P–Q3
7 0–0	0–0
8 P–K3	

White plans to shut the bishop out of the game with P–Q4. Karpov's next move prevents that advance by pinning the knight.

8 ...   **B–KN5**
9 P–KR3   **B×N**

A surprising decision, surrendering the bishop pair and leaving the white bishop in uncontested control of the white squares, but 9 ... B–R4 10 P–KN4 B–N3 11 P–Q4 is favourable to White.

10 B×B   N×N
11 P×N   N–K2
12 P–N3   Q–Q2
13 B–KN2

White can be content with his position from the opening. He is ready to play B–QN2 and P–Q4 or P–B4, utilizing his bishops in conjunction with the advantage in space conferred by the pawn on Q5. Karpov decides to challenge that pawn, though he can only do so at the cost of opening the long white diagonal for Korchnoi's bishop.

13 ...   P–QB3
14 P×P   N×P
15 B–N2   P–Q4

If Black does not play this move, White has a clear advantage thanks to the powerful bishops. By taking control of the centre in this way, Black

can hope to stifle their effect. The move 15 ... P–Q4, however, allows Korchnoi a combination which wins a pawn.

16 B×KP!   N×B
17 P–Q4

Not only does this move regain the piece, but Black is left with a sickly pawn on Q4 which he loses by force. The only consolation is the presence of opposite-coloured bishops when the dust settles.

17 ...   B–Q3
18 P×N   B×P
19 R–B1   P–Q5

Attempting to defend the pawn with 19 ... QR–Q1? would allow simply 20 R–B5 winning it under better circumstances than in the game. Now 20 P×P B×QP is completely equal since 21 B×P would be met by 21 ... B×P+ and material stays level. Korchnoi has a better idea.

20 R–B5!

The final point of the combination begun with 16 B×KP. The double threat of R×B and R–Q5 ensures the gain of a pawn.

20 ...   B–B3

20 ... B–Q3 could have been met simply by 21 Q×P.

21 R–Q5   Q–B2
22 P×P   QR–Q1
23 Q–B1   Q–N3!
24 R×R   R×R
25 P–Q5   P–N3

By ensuring that the extra white pawn has had to advance to Q5, Karpov lessens the scope of White's bishop and makes it hard for White to form any coherent plan. Black will sit firmly on his Q3 to blockade the pawn. In such positions with queen, rook and opposite-coloured bishops,

an extra pawn generally only confers winning chances if the pawn formation is not static. If, for example, White's extra pawn were on K4, rather than Q5, with the bishop on Q5, he would have fine chances to win by developing an attack based on an advance of K-side pawns to KB4 and K5, gradually squashing Black into total passivity. With the pawn on Q5, his position is totally lacking in dynamic potential and already looks destined for a draw.

| 26 B–B3 | K–N2 |
| 27 R–K1 | R–Q2 |

| 28 Q–KB4 | R–K2 |
| 29 R×R | |

Consenting to the exchange of rook lessens White's winning prospects even further, but 29 R–Q1 B–K4 would have brought only problems. If White wanted to keep rooks on the board, the fault lay in his previous two moves.

29 . . .	B×R
30 K–N2	P–QR4
31 P–KR4	P–R4
32 B–K2	B–B4
33 B–B4	Q–KB3
34 Q–Q2	

There is absolutely nothing for White to do, with or without queens on the board. The game meanders peacefully to its conclusion.

34 . . .	P–N3
35 P–R4	Q–K4
36 Q–Q3	Q–B3
37 Q–Q2	Q–K4
38 B–K2	Q–K5+
39 B–B3	Q–K4
40 B–Q1	Q–K5+

The game was adjourned here and **agreed drawn** without resumption.

Game Sixteen

Korchnoi and his seconds began work at 9.30 in the morning of this game rather than their usual 12.30. They had much work to do to repair the damage of game fourteen. 5-2 down and with the black pieces is a dangerous situation. Should he play the same line as in game fourteen or take the equally risky path of a change of opening? Korchnoi adopted the brave course of following the route which led to disaster. His decision was justified by the opening which went well for Black, but in time-trouble again Korchnoi erred and the adjourned position looked dubious. Some predicted an immediate end to the match. Adjournment analysis, aided by a fine sealed move, led to Korchnoi's salvation. The Soviet analysts had reached the same conclusion and Karpov did not press his claims at the second session. So Korchnoi lived to fight another day and the deputy minister of sport had to wait for his celebrations.

White: Karpov
Black: Korchnoi
Ruy Lopez

1 P–K4	P–K4
2 N–KB3	N–QB3
3 B–N5	P–QR3
4 B–R4	N–B3
5 0–0	N×P
6 P–Q4	P–QN4
7 B–N3	P–Q4
8 P×P	B–K3
9 QN–Q2	N–B4
10 P–B3	P–Q5
11 B×B	N×B
12 P×P	QN×QP
13 N–K4	B–K2

Played this time without the luxury of seventy-eight minutes' thought.

14 B–K3	N–KB4!

116

At last an improvement on game fourteen. Black offers an exchange of queens, while also threatening to disrupt White's pawns by taking the bishop.

15 Q–B2

An interesting solution. Now 15 . . . N×B is met by 16 Q–B6+ K–B1 17 P×N when the displaced black king has problems.

15 . . .	0–0

16 N(K4)–N5

16 N–B6+ B×N 17 Q×N B–K2 is not bad for Black. His knight neutralizes any attacking ambitions of the white knight, and Black's Q-side majority of pawns can roll forward strongly.

| 16 . . . | B×N |
| 17 N×B | P–N3! |

A fine move showing a deep understanding of the position. Instead 17 . . . N×N 18 Q×N would have been much better for White, whose KB-pawn will quickly advance with strong threats against the K-side. Now Black threatens at last to take the bishop since the mate threat on KR7 has disappeared.

| 18 N×N | P×N |

Black's handling of the opening has left him with firm control of the white squares and a knight which is potentially superior to the white bishop. In compensation, White can hope to take advantage of weaknesses on the black Q-side. The position is more or less equal.

19 QR–K1

19 B–B5 looks far more natural.

19 . . .	Q–Q4
20 P–QN3	QR–B1
21 B–B5	KR–Q1
22 P–KR3	Q–B3!

Pinning the bishop and introducing such possibilities as R–Q4 or N–Q5.

23 P–QN4	R–Q2
24 R–Q1	QR–Q1
25 R×R	R×R
26 R–K1	Q–Q4

Now with control of the open file and even more white squares to play with Black has a pleasant position. White must create another open file to give his rook or queen chances to penetrate the black position. The main positive feature of the white pieces is a potential attack on the black squares round the enemy king.

| 27 P–QR4! | N–R5 |
| 28 P–B3 | N–B4 |

Having induced the weakness, the knight returns.

29 P×P	P×P
30 Q–K2	Q–B3
31 R–QB1	R–Q1
32 B–K3	Q–Q4
33 B–B2	

Not 33 R×P? when 33 . . . Q×KP wins a piece.

| 33 . . . | P–B3 |

With his pawn majority held up by White's firm control of his QB5, Black finds it hard to formulate a plan.

| 34 Q–K1 | Q–N6 |
| 35 R–R1 | |

35 R×P? R–Q8 would have lost the white queen.

35 . . .	Q–N7
36 R–N1	Q–R7
37 R–Q1	R–Q4
38 R×R	BP×R

Finally Black has achieved something. The threats of infiltration by queen and rook have forced White to exchange and give Black a supported passed pawn. Karpov must seek counterplay on the K-side quickly.

39 P–N4   N–N2?

A time-trouble decision which is hard to understand. After 39 . . . N–K2, the knight is well placed to come to QB3, molesting the QN-pawn and K-pawn. The knight is superior to White's bishop and should be used actively. Korchnoi's curious retreat gives White time to develop a sudden, and very threatening initiative. Perhaps he feared 39 . . . N–K2 40 B–B5 N–B3 41 Q–K3 with the white queen threatening to come to KB4 or KR6 and threaten mate on B8, but even if Black has to retreat with Q–R1 he still has a good game.

40 B–B5   P–R3
41 Q–K3

The adjourned position, and one

which led to much expressed pessimism for Korchnoi's prospects. As he shows, however, it is not so bad.

41 . . .   Q–B7!

41 . . . P–R4 42 Q–B4 would indeed have been bad for Black. White has plans including a mating attack with Q–B6 and B–B8, while his king can run away from checks by the black queen by heading for KN5 if necessary. By refusing to take notice of the attack on his KR-pawn, Korchnoi eases his defence.

42 K–B1

A tacit compliment to Korchnoi's sealed move. Karpov refuses to test the complications of 41 Q×P P–Q5! when 42 B×P loses a piece to 42 . . . Q–Q8+, while other moves allow the pawn to reach Q6 with dangerous threats.

42 . . .   P–N4
    Agreed drawn.

White gains nothing with 43 P–R4 P×P 44 Q×P Q–Q8+ 45 K–B2 Q–B7+, while other attempts to breach the black K-side also leave the white king exposed to too many checks from the black queen. Adjournment analysis must have convinced Karpov that playing for a win was too dangerous.

Game Seventeen

The dullest game of the match. Korchnoi seemed to decide early in the game that it was time for a rest. For the first time, he did not open 1 P–QB4, perhaps to prevent the same defence to the English which Karpov had adopted in game fifteen. Karpov responded to Korchnoi's variation in order by an early transposition back to the Queen's Gambit. Lots of exchanges and a quick draw.

White: Korchnoi
Black: Karpov
Queen's Gambit Declined

1 N–KB3	N–KB3
2 P–B4	P–K3
3 N–QB3	P–Q4

Karpov is happy with a Queen's Gambit today, because the present move order precludes the variation chosen in game thirteen.

4 P–Q4	B–K2
5 B–N5	P–KR3
6 B–R4	0–0
7 R–B1	P×P
8 P–K3	P–B4
9 B×P	P×P
10 N×P	

Varying from the 10 P×P which had led to such a disaster in game nine, but this symmetrical continuation offers prospects only of a dull draw.

10 . . .	B–Q2
11 B–K2	N–B3
12 N–N3	N–Q4
13 B×B	

13 N×N B×B would be good for Black.

13 . . .	N(B3)×B
14 N×N	N×N
15 Q–Q4	B–B3
16 B–B3	N–K2
17 B×B	N×B
18 Q×Q	KR×Q
19 K–K2	QR–B1
20 P–QR3	K–B1
21 R–B2	N–K2
22 KR–QB1	R×R+
23 R×R	K–K1

Agreed drawn.

119

Game Eighteen

With a fine sense of occasion, Karpov produced his best game of the whole match to put an end to the contest. In game fourteen he had already produced an important improvement in the Ruy Lopez. Today he played an improvement on his own improvement! From the opening, Korchnoi was struggling and the World Champion never let his grip slacken. When the game was adjourned, it was only a question of when Korchnoi would telephone his resignation. Anatoly Karpov was Chess Champion of the World for another three years.

White: Karpov
Black: Korchnoi

1	P–K4	P–K4		
2	N–KB3	N–QB3		
3	B–N5	P–QR3		
4	B–R4	N–B3		
5	0–0	N×P		

Of course one may criticize Korchnoi for persevering with this defence, but games are lost by poor play rather than choice of opening. The curious feature of his play with the black pieces was the decision to play Petroff's Defence and the Berlin Defence in the early games, when he was apparently trying to win games with Black, then switching to the Open Defence later, when the state of the match made it more sensible to play for draws. Petroff's Defence and the Berlin are solid equalizing attempts; the Open is a win-or-lose choice.

6	P–Q4	P–QN4
7	B–N3	P–Q4

8	P×P	B–K3
9	QN–Q2	N–B4
10	P–B3	P–Q5
11	B×B	N×B
12	P×P	QN×QP
13	P–QR4!	

This immediate molestation of the black Q-side pawns creates considerable extra strain on the black position.

13 . . .	B–K2

120

After 13 . . . R–QN1 14 P×P P×P
15 N–K4 we have a similar position to
those of the earlier games, but with
White in possession of the QR-file.
Nevertheless, that looks better for
Black than what happens in the
game.

14 N×N!   **N×N**

14 . . . Q×N 15 P×P wins a pawn
for White.

15 N–K4

Now this knight move is more effective than on move thirteen. White's
threat is 16 P×P, when Black cannot
recapture with the pawn without losing his knight after R×R.

15 . . .   **N–K3**
16 B–K3   **0–0**
17 P–B4

The K-side majority of pawns is
White's major trump. White cannot
be allowed to play P–B5 and P–B6 in
the middlegame, but the endgame is
also no pleasure for Black.

17 . . .   **Q×Q**
18 KR×Q   **KR–N1**

Hoping for counterplay down the
QN-file, but 18 . . . KR–Q1 was
better.

19 R–Q7   **B–B1**
20 P–B5   **N–Q1**

21 P–R5!

Cutting out any Black counterchances based on . . . P×P, Karpov
completes his bind on the whole position. Now Black has all his pieces on
the back rank, weaknesses on QB2
and QR3 and still those rampant
white K-side pawns with which to
cope.

21 . . .   **N–B3**
22 P–K6!   **P×P**
23 P–B6!

Since 23 . . . P×P leads to mate after
24 N×P+ K–R1 25 R×RP Black
has to allow the continued existence
of the dangerous white pawn on B6.

23 . . .   **N–K4**
24 R×P   **R–B1**
25 QR–B1   **R×R**
26 R×R   **R–Q1**

By giving back his extra pawn, Korchnoi has at last managed to create a
glimmer of activity. He threatens N–
N5 and R–Q8, but that is easily dealt
with. Note that 26 . . . N–N5 27 P–
B7+ K–R1 28 B–B5 would also have
been miserable for Black.

27 P–R3   **P–R3**
28 R–R7

Finally the black QR-pawn, fixed
with White's 21 P–R5, comes in for
some attention.

28 . . .   **N–B5**
29 B–N6   **R–N1**
30 B–B5!

After 30 R×P N×NP Black can
struggle; the QR-pawn will not go
away, so Karpov increases his advantage still further. The threat is simply
31 B×B and 32 R×NP with a killing
passed KB-pawn.

30 . . .   **B×B+**

30 . . . N×NP is most elegantly met
by 31 B–Q4 with P×P to follow.

31 N×B   **P×P**

121

32 P–QN4!
Safeguarding both white Q-side pawns and ensuring the death of Black's.

32 . . .	R–Q1
33 R×P	K–B2
34 R–R7+	K–N3
35 R–Q7!	

The manner in which Karpov allows not the vestige of a chance to his opponent is highly impressive. Now 35 . . . R×R 36 N×R would leave Black unable to stop the QR-pawn.

35 . . .	R–K1
36 P–R6	R–QR1
37 R–QN7	K–B4

Or 37 . . . N–Q3 38 R–N6 winning a pawn or two.

38 R×P	K–K4
39 R–N7	K–Q4
40 R–KB7	P–B4
41 R–B6	

Having lured the black king to the Q-side in order to stop the advance of the pawns, Karpov looks for pickings on the defenceless other wing.

The final position of the 1981 World Championship match. One pawn down and with more to follow, Black has nothing to play for. A sad end to a generally unhappy match for the challenger.

Black resigned.

Postscript

World Chess Champion Anatoly Karpov looked contented and confident at his press conference after the match. He had retained his title by the convincing margin of six games to two with ten draws. He had trained for a longer match and still seemed strong. In reply to questions he spoke highly of his opponent's chessplaying abilities, avoiding any further slurs on his character. There was no longer any need for that; the battle was over. Karpov had indeed sent a 'mission accomplished' telegram to Leonid Brezhnev, just as he had done after his victory three years ago, just as Botvinnik had cabled Stalin in 1936. The protocol, as well as the sentiments expressed and phraseology used, have changed little in those years.

Karpov's victory, however, has been well deserved. His ability to withstand the intense pressure of such a match has been impressively demonstrated. Not since Capablanca's defeat of Lasker can a contestant in a World Championship match have made so few identifiable errors in the games. His practical approach, intense preparation and above all his perfectly controlled temperament, mark Karpov as a formidable match opponent and a great World Champion. Shortly after he succeeded to that title, Karpov was asked whom he considered to be his most dangerous rivals. He replied, with impressive objectivity, that he did not see anyone who might be a serious threat. Now, with two successful title defences to his credit, it is perhaps still more difficult to see anyone who might be a challenge to his supremacy.

For challenger Viktor Korchnoi, much bitterness still remains. At the closing ceremony in Merano, he was not invited to share the stage with the organizers and his conqueror. Even his runner-up's award was brought down to his table in the body of the hall. Korchnoi was insulted and refused to attend the celebration final dinner. His feelings towards Karpov have not been eased by the cessation of hostilities. In an interview after the match he said that the Central Intelligence Agency had offered to help him. 'If I had to play him again I would apply for their services.' But the precise nature of those services was not specified.

For Korchnoi, the battle seems lost. It is difficult to believe that he can win through to challenge Karpov yet again, or indeed that he would really want to. In Merano, he seemed to have lost not only the match, he had also lost heart. He had set out not just to win, but to destroy Karpov, a task he knew to be beyond him. From the very start Korchnoi and his followers looked as though they expected to lose. Perhaps he simply felt three years older than in Baguio City. Yet we must remember that Emanuel Lasker scored some impressive triumphs in his sixties. Let us all hope that Viktor Korchnoi can come to terms with himself after this defeat and emulate the feats of longevity of that great player.

Let us hope too that the Soviet authorities show some magnanimity in victory. If Bella and Igor Korchnoi can soon be allowed to join Viktor, then the whole affair could still end with some dignity.